Donbas

Donbas

A True Story of
an Escape Across Russia

Jacques Sandulescu

AN AUTHORS GUILD BACKINPRINT.COM EDITION

Donbas
A True Story of an Escape Across Russia
All Rights Reserved © 1968, 2000 by Jacques Sandulescu

AN AUTHORS GUILD BACKINPRINT.COM EDITION

Published by iUniverse.com, Inc.

For information address:
iUniverse.com, Inc.
5220 S 16th, Ste. 200
Lincoln, NE 68512
www.iuniverse.com

Originally published by David McKay Co. Inc.

ISBN: 0-595-15043-8

Printed in the United States of America

Book I

Chapter I

I WAS ARRESTED in Brasov on my way to school. It was just beginning to get light, and the cold dark-gray streets were almost empty. At a corner near the school grounds I saw several armed Russian soldiers and a Romanian civilian interpreter shoving somebody into a police truck. They saw me, and the interpreter shouted:

"Where are you going?"

"To school."

"Come, we have to take you somewhere, then afterwards you can go to school."

He grabbed me, and the soldiers helped him push me toward the truck. I shook free and jumped in by myself. It was pitch dark inside, but I could feel several people watching me.

We were taken to the Axa movie house. It was jammed with people milling about the aisles. Some were sitting down, and it looked very strange, since there was no movie. I looked around in vain for someone

I knew. An intense feeling of uncertainty and fear was in the air. No one asked any questions about what was happening. The answers were lying in the pit of everyone's stomach, but we were all trying to ignore them for fear of making them come true. Everyone made himself as inconspicuous as possible, moving quietly, speaking softly, making no gestures. Fear suspended feeling, thought, movement.

I stood around waiting vaguely for a long time, but no one spoke to me. I took a seat, pulled my head down into my shoulders, and thought about the many times I had sat in the same theater enjoying an afternoon film. My thoughts went back, back, back...then I remember wondering idly what movie would be shown next.

A few hours later, an interpreter got up on the stage and said in a loud voice that we would be loaded into trucks and taken to barracks on the outskirts of town. There was one truck and one street bus, and they made about ten trips each. In the barracks people started crying and praying and generally making a lot of noise. Some were singing hymns. Toward evening we were taken in more trucks to the railroad station, where we were transferred to a train of thirty boxcars. We went into the cars from the back, because in front on the station platform there was an enormous crowd. We were counted as we went in. There were forty-six of us, men and women, in my car.

About fifteen yards from the train, masses of screaming and crying people were being held back by a cordon of Russian guards. After a lot of pushing, I had a turn at one of the two small windows. I saw my father right away—tall, a whole head above the sea of people. I whistled sharply. He saw me immediately and made his way through the crowd until he was straight across from me. Our eyes met and held. I saw and felt him fighting tears back—I had never seen him this way before. I tried to look confident so he would know I could take care of myself. After two minutes I was roughly shoved away by others who were also searching for a familiar face. As soon as I was away from the window, the tears came. My only consolation was knowing that my father couldn't see me crying. It would have been too hard for him. Through my tears I could see the people pushing at the window, waving frantically and trying to shout something to their friends and relatives outside, wringing their hands and weeping. Then with a heave the train started to move, and a high-pitched wailing arose from the boxcars and from the crowd outside.

I was sixteen, and I turned out to be the youngest prisoner in my boxcar, but I wasn't the smallest, for I stood six feet two and weighed a hundred and eighty pounds. In the car there were two engineers, a doctor, and the brother of one of the professors at my preparatory school. Most of the other prisoners I had either seen occasionally in the street or had heard about. It struck me as strange that neither the doctor nor the engineers did anything to establish any kind of order among these howling people. As men of standing, they should at least have tried to console them, especially the wailing women, who were making the most noise. Already I was beginning to lose my respect for people. I thought they were all terribly weak.

The image of my father kept coming before my eyes, but I forced myself to put it out of my mind and sat down in a corner so that I could think about my situation. There was no one that I knew well enough to talk to about it, and I felt terribly alone amid all this chaos.

Despite everything, there still seemed to be a spark of hope that the train's destination might not be a Soviet slave labor camp. But hope is hope, and reason is reason. I decided that no matter where they shipped us, other people lived and worked there. It would just be a matter of adjusting. Then I thought about escape. I had read books and heard stories about escapes from prison camps, and my head was full of ideas about tunnels and hundreds of different ways to fool guards and police. I would have to wait and see.

I was very curious about the Soviet Union. Lately we had been hearing a lot of good things about it. It was the beginning of 1945, and Russian troops had occupied Romania for the past four months. Romania had been an ally of Germany and had suddenly switched sides when the Russians started coming across the border with the German army retreating before them. The troops in Brasov were wild. In the evenings the soldiers would roam the streets, drinking and singing. They looted stores, and they would light fires in the middle of the street and cook stolen chickens. Some of the soldiers were women, and one of them went walking around one evening wearing silk pajamas that she had bought in an expensive lingerie shop. Everyone thought she was insane, and finally someone told her that they were only for sleeping. I gathered that they didn't have such luxuries in Russia. Still, it was supposed to be a workers' paradise.

My thoughts were interrupted by sharp hunger. Most of the prisoners had been arrested in their homes and had been able to bring some food, soap, towels, or clothing with them. All I had with me were three books—a Romanian history, a geography, and a German history. A little later, the brother of the professor offered me some bread and sausage. I said no, thank you, but later on in the night he offered me some again, and I was very glad to get something to eat. The next day the Russians started giving us rations of bread and soup.

It was January and bitter cold. A small iron stove supplied with a small ration of coal was our only source of warmth, and the cold poured in through hundreds of cracks in the walls. We slept in shifts. On each side of the car two levels of wooden slabs accommodated about twenty people. When one person turned over, his five bedmates had to turn over also. It was the kind of sleep you catch sitting up on long bus or train rides. What it really amounted to was taking the weight off your feet for six hours. After that you got so fidgety that you couldn't stand it any longer and had to get up and walk around.

In three days we got to the Russian border and had to transfer to another train, because the gauge of the rails is different in Russia. The two trains were side by side about thirty feet away from each other, and the prisoners were transferred a car at a time. I thought of hiding under the bunks, but when our car was emptied we were counted as we went out, and I saw guards checking inside the cars before us. We were left in the Russian train overnight, and the next morning at sunrise we started off. The train crawled up a hill and around a bend, and through the window I could see the engine way up ahead of us. It was a very long train. At some station where we had stopped, they must have added another forty to fifty boxcars. I wondered where we were headed. The land was flat and desolate, mile after mile of it. Occasionally we would pass a small village with empty snow-covered fields around it.

At one stop during the first week, we were given an axe for half an hour and allowed to chop a small hole in the floor near the door. Instead of people defecating out the window by sticking their behinds out while two others held a blanket for privacy, one could now use the hole behind the shelter of the blanket. Urinating was no problem for the men, as the sliding door had a large crack in it. When a woman or a girl needed to urinate, the blanket had to be held again.

During the second week, while we were snowed in on a siding, several of the men started to play cards. After trying several games, they decided to stick with "21." Something about the finality of the game must have appealed to them. It was fascinating to watch them. The atmosphere immediately changed from that of a prison transport to that of a gambling house. For a while everyone crowded around the players, whispering about this or that hand, and for the first time in a week there was a place free by the stove. I opened its little door and watched the coal glowing and burning with blue flames. With some astonishment I realized that I had never seen coal burn before. Then I was again a small boy at home on the long winter evenings, with logs blazing in the huge fireplace, with my giant of a father and my mother and sister. A voice broke my thoughts…

"Close the oven door, kid, it'll burn better."

I closed the door and gave up my place to someone else.

For lack of any other diversion, I soon became interested in the card game. Their stakes were getting very high. It happened that I had 20,000 *lei*, or about 165 dollars (peacetime), in my pocket, which I had earned on the so-called black market. I had been one of the many young boys taking advantage of the crazy opportunities that inflation creates in wartime, particularly in occupied countries. Since the Russians had captured Brasov a few months before, I had overheard hundreds of conversations in school about trading with the Russian officers. One boy had been given 30,000 *lei* for his bicycle. It seemed like an enormous amount of money, although almost everything cost at least a hundred times its normal price. Normally a bicycle sold for 1,000 *lei*.

I heard that the officer who had bought the bicycle was looking for an accordion. This was a piece of luck, for I had a fine accordion that my father had given my for my fourteenth birthday. I figured that if I could sell it for a lot of money I would easily be able to replace it and still have a tidy sum left over. I approached the officer in question and made a deal right away for 100,000 *lei*. It was mostly in 100-and 500-*lei* silver coins, and it took me an hour to count them. I hid 80,000 at home and was still waiting to decide what to do when I was arrested with the rest in my pockets. But during the four-or five-day interval I'd been plagued by guilt feelings, because I hadn't consulted my parents beforehand. I thought that if I showed them a bigger accordion plus 80,000 *lei* they would congratulate me, but I couldn't be sure.

After thinking about this and fingering the money in my pocket for a while, I decided to try my luck. I won and lost and won again. At one point I drew 18 and put all my money on the table. Three rounds later I had 400,000 *lei*. I quickly lost most of it, and then I won back even more and ended up with 500,000 *lei*. Under ordinary circumstances I would have been very happy, but as I looked at the money I doubted that it would do me any good in Russia, for they would probably take our possessions away when we arrived.

After the game was over, a woman began to hum a sad, depressing church hymn. Another woman picked it up, and soon a general gloom hung over the car, but two of the livelier gamblers saved the night by singing some bawdy tavern songs. In the midst of this bedlam I dozed off.

Every second or third day we would stop and the guards would let a few people out to get food and water. Each boxcar was allowed two pails of water, and each group of five persons shared a loaf of bread a day. In addition, some thin cabbage soup and kasha (buckwheat porridge) were distributed. I always volunteered for these details because they gave me a little relief from the constant weeping. I just had to get away, even though the snow was knee high and I was wearing a pair of low black shoes. By the time I got back to the car my feet would be soaked. After a week the shoes turned white and started to crack around the edges. I began to worry, imagining what it would be like being barefoot for the rest of the winter.

Details were especially worthwhile when we stopped at small villages or towns. As we marched to the food station I studied the people we saw, since according to Communist propaganda we had entered the Labor Paradise. But I saw nothing except ragged-looking people who spat on us at every opportunity. Some of the men were so accomplished at this sport that despite the fact that I was on the receiving end I was forced to admire their skill. But at first I was puzzled as to why we were hated so. Gradually I realized that to these people prisoners represented the enemy who had plundered and devastated their land. So in their helpless anger they literally spat out their hatred. Those who hated the most spat the worst—for as usual, emotion fouled things up.

Every chance I got, I would go to the window of the car and look out on the vast flat country. It wasn't divided into squares by fences and roads the way most of Europe is. As far as the eye could see, there was nothing but snow-covered plains.

The trip lasted three weeks. Darkness would take over around three-thirty or four in the afternoon. Sometimes we were left on a siding for as long as two or three days. The cold was terrible, and shivering drained our energy. My teeth would chatter all night long. In the morning, exhausted by this continual tenseness, I would try to get my blood circulating by moving around. But everybody else would be doing the same thing, and our bodies would constantly bump. I could hardly wait for work details, even though my feet took a beating every time I went out into the snow. The endless standing around, shifting your weight from one foot to the other, sitting occasionally, sleeping hardly at all— hour after hour, day after day—was too much to bear.

The thing that most jangled my nerves was the loud praying of these already beaten people. Oh, how they prayed. They prayed to the Lord, to Jesus Christ and Sweet Mary to help them, to take them back home. But no one seemed to hear, because slowly but surely we rolled on deeper and deeper into Russia until one day we crossed the huge Dnieper River. I had a five-minute look at Dniepropetrovsk; it was a large city separated east and west by the river. The city looked just like the people—shaggy, ugly, broken, gray.

Chapter II

ONE SNOWY MORNING the train stopped on a siding. In the distance, stretching some twenty miles all around us, were small hills of coal completely barren of snow. About half a mile away I saw some long, low barracks surrounded by a high wooden and barbed-wire fence. We had arrived.

It was late in the afternoon before they began unloading our boxcar. The sliding doors were opened and three heavily armed guards motioned us to get out. The men jumped down first and helped the women from the high car. Everyone was shaky after having been cramped up for three weeks.

When I reached the ground, I looked back to help the next woman. She turned out to be an epileptic who had been having five or six attacks a day during the long trip. She jumped into my waiting arms, and just as I was placing her safely on the ground, she began foaming at the mouth and making guttural, inhuman noises. I tried to get rid of her by laying her down in the snow, but a guard kicked me. I understood from this that I was to continue holding her. Meanwhile, everyone else fell into single file and marched off toward the barracks. I was getting tired, so I crouched down with the squirming woman in my arms. After a complete attack of contorted jerks, moans, and drooling, she finally came out of it. When I told her to get up, she refused until I shook her by the shoulders a few times. She staggered to her feet and made an effort to follow the column of prisoners, but she was so shaky that I had to support her all the way.

We moved slowly, and our long thin column looked like a black snake, crawling and winding through the cold white snow. Some of the people were struggling with suitcases, and although I was still support-ing the epileptic I was given a suitcase to carry also. My only possessions consisted of my three schoolbooks, which I now clutched very hard, and a spoon a woman in the train had given me.

Our camp consisted of twenty-one bleak wooden barracks, in three rows. There was no kitchen, no washroom, no toilets, and no bathhouse. The compound was surrounded on all sides by barbed wire.

We entered the camp through the guard shack. Inside, two officers counted us as we passed. From there we followed a path leading to the barracks. The snow was ankle deep and the drifts were shoulder high in some spots. The angry wind howled, biting and stinging and bringing tears to our eyes.

The first of the barracks buildings was about 88 yards long; thin clay walls separated it into eight compartments, four on each side. We were met by seven or eight growling guards who counted us again as we went in. They looked like Mongols, and they kicked us freely and fre-quently. I was kicked into the last room or compartment. Inside at the far end stood a little fireplace with some coal in it.

When we first came in, the barracks seemed warm, but after a while we felt chilly again. The only actual difference between inside and out-side was the lack of wind and the heat generated by our bodies; since we didn't have any wood, we couldn't light a fire. That night, sleep was out of the question. Those who hadn't brought blankets with them had to sleep on the hard dirt floor. It was a nightmare of crying, complaining, and praying. Couldn't these people realize that they were only making our situation worse?

Somehow morning came. All during the railroad trip I had been frightened by the uncertainty of what lay ahead, but that first morning I was especially anxious, for I realized that what we were supposed to do was now more important than where we were. My thoughts were interrupted by the arrival of a guard and an interpreter. The interpreter announced that men were needed for the following work details: bringing bread from a nearby town and distributing a loaf to every five prisoners, digging a latrine, building a kitchen, and unloading boards and pipes that were to be made into bunks. Then he asked for carpenters, and several men volunteered.

My job was digging the latrine with three other men. I had no gloves, and my shoes didn't protect me from the snow. I cried as my hands began to freeze, and the tears froze, too. In frustration I worked furiously with the pick, hoping to build up a little warmth.

It took us three days to finish the latrine. Each evening after work our reward was a fifth of a loaf of bread. The only thing we could look forward to after that was the next day's distribution. It's amazing how quickly people's reasons for pleasure can be simplified. Waiting for bread after work became the greatest joy on earth. It came fresh from the bak-ery in large canvas bags, and the saliva gathered thickly in our mouths as the odor pervaded the barracks. We would be herded into a corner of one of the rooms, while the opposite corner was stacked up to the ceiling with bread. Our eyes ate every crumb. Each of us imagined in his own way what he would do if an entire bakery fell to his disposal. During the first few weeks such daydreams kept me alive as much as anything else.

It took about twenty days of heavy work before the camp functioned with even a semblance of organization. They were painful weeks with painful lessons. In my compartment there was a blacksmith who had been arrested with his eighteen-year-old son. He was a tremendously powerful man; huge biceps and forearms would flex at us when he took off his shirt to look for lice. It made me laugh a little to see this powerhouse of a man scanning his body for tiny insects. But when he found them it was no laughing matter, for he would kill them with the same vengeance and lust that it takes to kill a man. Once, after we had received our rations, the blacksmith ate his up fast. He just devoured it. The he snatched half of his son's bread. When his son complained, he slapped him, with a terribly swift, catlike motion. The son cried quietly, but kept his mouth shut. I was stunned. Father and son. My father and me. If hunger could get the best of a man's paternal instincts, it could do worse. It was each one of us for himself. No relationships here, no room for the heart.

People were dying already; there was a regular burial detail, and the men assigned to it complained bitterly. One man in particular complained and complained. Finally I asked him, "Don't you think everyone is working hard? What are you crying about?"

"You don't understand," he said. "It's not the work. It's that we're digging graves for people who came with us from home. Today I dig a hole for somebody or other, and tomorrow who knows who's going to dig a hole for me, or for you? How long are we going to last?"

"But what good does your complaining do?" I asked him. "Try to put it out of your mind. I'm sure we weren't brought here to dig latrines until there's no one left to use them, and dig graves until we've all buried ourselves. When the camp functions, we're going to have to work somewhere, and if you keep complaining and worrying you'll just wear yourself out and tomorrow they'll dig your grave and that'll be that. You're better off saving your energy and staying alive."

He gave me a funny look and said, "How can you be so hard?" but he didn't complain any more after that.

One morning, three weeks after we had arrived, four officers and three civilians wearing fur coats came into our barracks with an interpreter. The civilians were party members and bore themselves with an air of superiority. We were told that we were in the greatest anthracite coal region in the world, the Donbas. We were to work in the mines as slave laborers. From school I remembered that the Donbas region covered many square miles of the Don valley in southern Russia. Hundreds of coal mines were scattered all through the area.

We were to be divided into three shifts: 7 A.M. to 3 P.M.; 3 P.M. to 11 P.M.; 11 P.M. to 7 A.M. Men and women would be treated the same. Also Stalin had passed a law to provide everyone, regardless of nationality, working underground in the Soviet Union with a thousand grams of bread a day. So far we had been getting about three hundred. Everyone working outside the mine—that is, on the platform surrounding the entrance—would get seven hundred grams. They told us that the soups would become richer and the kasha thicker and more abundant. We

would be issued new clothes when we needed them. In general, everything would improve, since we were in the workers' paradise.

A day or so later, as I was passing through the guard shack coming
back from a water detail, a young Russian officer spoke to me in a
friendly way. I didn't understand what he was saying, but from his gestures I understood that I was to give my two pails of water to two of the
older men who carried only one and come closer to him. I was limping
badly at the time, because my socks were rotted and full of holes and my
shoes were beginning to fall off my feet. The officer told me to take my
shoes off. When he saw the state of my feet, he shook his head and said,
"Yakoy numer?" several times. I understood that he wanted to know my
shoe size and drew the number 48 with my finger in the ashes next to
the little iron stove. The officer made a phone call and then went out,
saying *"Podasdi* [wait]." He went off in the direction of the officers'
quarters. Thirty minutes later he came back carrying a pair of brand-
new felt boots. He motioned for me to try them on. They fit perfectly.
I took them off and went outside to wash my sore, dirty feet in the snow.
Back in the shack I started to put my old shoes and socks on again, but
the officer gestured emphatically to take the felt boots. They were mine.

I couldn't believe it. I thanked him, almost in tears, and he said to me
"Vanya budish [you shall be Vanya]." It was to remain my name. Never in
my life have I felt so much gratitude. The boots looked so new and clean I
didn't even want to wear them. They were warm and comfortable, and
walking in deep snow became a pleasure. I loved them, and I loved that
officer. He was the first decent human being I had met since I had left
Romania. But it wasn't long before he was transferred, because he didn't
approve of the unnecessary hardships and beatings and often stopped the
sadistic guards from torturing and harassing the prisoners. He had a stern

face and steel-blue eyes, and he seldom smiled. I think the other officers were afraid of him and arranged to have him sent away.

That night there was a terrible snowstorm. The wind howled and whined like the song of the devil. Everyone slept badly. The next day the storm continued. I was sent out on a water detail. It was murderous in that wind. After a while I lost the feeling in my ears, face, and hands. But my feet were warm and comfortable. That night they brought in a half-frozen guard. He had been drinking and had stumbled and fallen on his way from the guards' quarters; two hours later they found him almost dead. They brought him into our barracks, which was closest to where he had fallen. When he came to, he started crying, and through his tears he cursed all the prisoners lying in their bunks. We became afraid of the wind, wondering what it would do to us, when in two hours it had almost killed a well-fed guard in a fur coat.

The next day the entire camp was marched out to Mine 31, about two miles away, to dig out the railroad tracks. A train of full coal cars was snowed in on a siding. Coming out of the siding, the tracks went through a low valley where in some places the drifts were ten and twelve feet high. Looking at the bright snow became painful.

That evening we were told that the following day we would be divided into shifts to work at several mines in the area. I looked forward to the change anxiously, because my rations would triple and also because it would take me away from the miserable camp.

Chapter III

I WAS ASSIGNED to the afternoon shift at Mine 89, a long way from the barracks. On the way we passed an enormous trench about twenty feet deep and twenty feet wide. Later I learned that it had been dug a few years back to delay the German tanks. It was hundreds of miles long, and the ground was very rocky. I thought about the hours of sweat and labor that must have gone into it. I asked several Russians how it had been done. The reply was always the same: with pick and shovel. It reminded me of the great wall of China, which I had read about in school.

After walking for about an hour and a half we got to Mine 89. I was put to work on the *atkatka* platform, which was a small hill where the coal was unloaded. A winch with a long cable pulled two one-ton cars at a time out of the mine shaft, and then lowered two empty cars to replace them. The full cars were rolled onto the top of the coal hill, tipped over, and shoveled out. On the opposite side of the hill from the

mine shaft the coal was loaded into trucks that took it to the railroad at
Mine 31, seven and a half miles away.

I worked with a Russian girl and an older Russian unloading cars.
They both seemed to like me. I was the only prisoner on the *atkatka*.
The first day was long. My felt boots got all black, and I realized they
wouldn't last very long in the sharp-edged coal. The Russian workers all
had rubber shoes.

At the end of our shift, at 11:30 P.M., we walked back with a guard.
The night was crystal clear. There was no wind, just a dry, penetrating
cold. I gazed up at the sky. Millions of stars shone not very far away. The
stars were impersonal; only the bright moon looked a little friendlier.

Several weeks passed, and I began to lose track of time. My bread
rations were now seven hundred grams, or about twenty-five ounces, a
day. One afternoon a Russian worker from our shift was sick. Our foreman suggested that I take his place for eight hours. A lamp was hung
around my neck, and I joined the rest of the forty Russians and prisoners going down into the mine.

The shaft descended at a forty-five-degree angle, and I slipped and
fell many times. We finally got to the first level, where a tunnel ran off
horizontally in both directions. Some of the workers got off here, and
the rest of us continued our descent until we reached the second level.
We went into the tunnel to the right. It was very wet. I tried walking on
the rails where the cars rolled, but I slipped off them. Finally it made no
difference whether or not I stepped in dry places, because my feet were
soaked. The Russians had galoshes, and two or three of them even wore
rubber pants and jackets.

After a fifteen-minute walk we stopped. In the wall at about shoulder height was a hole, three feet square. A stream of water poured out of

it. Two of the Russians hoisted themselves up and crawled into it, and then it was my turn. Inside, the hole became a tunnel about ten feet wide and four feet high which ascended at a forty-five-degree angle. This level was called a *lava*. A jungle of braces held up the ceiling; in some places they were so close together we had trouble crawling between them. We climbed up about a hundred yards until we came to the point where the coal vein started.

I was handed a half-broken shovel. One of the Russians broke the coal down with a pick and crowbar, and I shoveled it into an open tin chute that ran down the length of the level. A Russian girl with a piece of rubber tied to her backside sat in the chute and pushed the wet coal with her feet, traveling down with it. When she got to the bottom, it fell into the car underneath the hole and she came back up and started over. It was a never-ending nightmare. Water dripped from everywhere. Since the level was only four feet high, I had to shovel the coal on my knees and heave it over my shoulder in a crippling position. One of the Russians put up new braces as we went along, and every once in a while I could lean against one of them, making it a little easier to work. I was wet right from the beginning.

At last our shift was over. As we went up, the Russians said I was a good worker. As soon as we came out into the cold, my wet clothes turned into ice. I was dead tired and my back hurt; I had bumped it several times trying to stand up in the mine. I was filthy and frozen. On the walk back to camp my feet became warm, and I tried to concentrate on them and forget the rest of my body. That night I made up my mind to escape as soon as I could.

About a week after that, two men did escape. Their names were Ion Steinger and Stephan Pivas. There was a lot of confusion. Three days later, when we got back from the night shift, we were told to wait in front of the barracks. The other prisoners were herded outside. An interpreter hollered, "You will see an example of what will happen to anyone who tries to escape."

It was just getting light. The commandant came out; he stood about fifty feet away from me while they dragged one prisoner out of the guard shack. He looked as if he'd been badly beaten. The other man had been killed when they were captured. The commandant told the prisoner to kneel down. Then he pulled out his pistol and shot him in the neck. The man fell over, and his legs kicked a couple of times.

I froze. It was so sudden. But perhaps he was lucky; no more cold, misery, hunger. I wondered vaguely: If I jump the commandant, will he shoot me immediately, or will he torture me first? The mere thought of torture sent shivers through me. On second thought I wanted very much to live, and get out of there. If I wanted to escape, it would have to be very carefully planned, and then carried out with absolute determination.

On the way back into the barracks a lot of the prisoners started crying and praying for the executed man's soul. A lot of good it did him…The Russians obviously meant business, and that was that. I slept badly. Every detail of the scene went through my mind a hundred times. But during the next few days, as I considered the episode more calmly, I decided that the two fellows had been very naive and inept. One had to be mad to try to escape in the winter, and without any knowledge of Russian. They had been nineteen and twenty-three years old. Result: two deaths. I made a mental note to learn Russian as fast as I could. Spring was only one or two months away, and summer would soon follow. Late in the summer I knew I could sleep in the fields…

Ion, Stephan, and I were planning the escape. I was confused. We planned it on the way home from the mine. Inside the camp we got our bread rations, volunteered for water detail, and just kept on going. Night fell. We walked through the night and decided that during the day we would lie low. We lay down in a young, green cornfield, but there was a foot of snow on the ground. I couldn't understand it. Peering out from behind the green stalks, I saw three guards walking toward the field, their rifles in their arms and a dog trotting behind them. Instead of doing something, I just lay down quietly and wondered why it was so cold and snowy on the ground when we were lying between green cornstalks. Then the guards' voices became louder and closer. I closed my eyes and thought about dying. I heard a click, and when I opened my eyes a rifle was pointing straight at my head from about two feet away. Stephan also had a rifle pointing at him. Behind the rifles were two savage, growling faces. I knew that Ion was already dead. Stephan tried to reach for the rifle and the growling of the guards grew louder and louder and...boom! Stephan's forehead had a round hole in it; blood oozed out of it over his eyes. They were still open, looking at me. The guards turned to me, raised their rifles...

I was in the cold, dark barracks.

We worked six days and had the seventh day off, but this turned out to be no great treat, for there were always innumerable details to which we were assigned. The worst detail—I had to agree with the old man— was burying the dead. Almost every day someone died, sometimes three or four in a day. The only remotely pleasant detail was distributing the bread ration. But after a while this was permanently in the hands of a few people who had managed to bring something valuable with them from home, such as a watch or a fur hat, which they gave to the officer in charge of our barracks or to the interpreter.

The only valuable thing I had turned out to be my books. Cigarettes were very expensive, and everyone smoked rough Mahorka tobacco rolled into pieces of old Pravda newspaper. One of the friendlier guards, who occasionally gave me a wink or slapped me on the back, was a heavy smoker, and one day as I was going through the guard shack on my way out on a water detail I saw him looking around for some paper. I remembered that I had the books and when I got back from the detail I went to my barracks and brought him my German history. He was immensely pleased, and a few days later he came into the barracks with a small satchel of cornmeal and asked me if I had any more paper. I gave him my geography book, and he ripped out about ten pages. Then he measured out three glassfuls of cornmeal into my cooking pot, thanked me, and left. I boiled the cornmeal with water and a little salt, and it was very filling. The books provided me with cornmeal every few days for several weeks, until there was nothing left but the covers.

There was a very pretty and fiery eighteen-year-old girl in one of the women's compartments in our barracks. She was from one of the better families at home. Our interpreter wanted to seduce her, but she insulted him when he propositioned her. Some people said that she had slapped him, but I found that hard to believe. In any case, a few days later the officer in charge asked for her, and she went off with him to his quarters. Ten minutes later she ran back crying hysterically, "Never, never will I submit to a Russian officer." The next day she was assigned to work in Mine 89. She came along with our shift. At the mine she was told that she would be working inside, on the second level. I could picture her sitting in the cold, dirty chute, pushing the wet, mud-like coal with her her feet. It made me shiver. Just before she went down, she asked me what it was like. I lacked the heart to tell her and just shrugged my shoulders.

Eight hours later, she came up changed from a girl into a black body. The tears had made gray streaks on her black face. She must have cried the entire eight hours. She wouldn't speak; she just looked straight ahead and marched off with the rest of us. Back in camp, she immediately went to see the officer. They agreed that she would be permanently assigned to a kitchen job, and in return, every few days she would visit the officer's quarters. I didn't blame her, but I hated that rotten interpreter. She could not have survived more than a few weeks in Mine 89. Now she might outlast us all.

A few weeks later at Mine 31 I saw a Romanian woman on her first day at the mine who was unable to unload a car of slag. The Russian foreman kicked her a few times in the rear and was cursing her, calling her a lazy parasite, when one of the prisoners who had just finished his shift inside the mine came up, took the shovel out of her hand, and unloaded the car for her. The prisoner was one of the best workers. The foreman and several other Russians stood and watched him, amazed. Then they started laughing and making fun of him. It seemed ridiculous to them that this man who had just finished working for eight hours should help a woman who to them wasn't worth the bread she consumed. In Russia the women worked like the men and had the same rights. I remembered the Russian woman in Brasov who had never seen silk pajamas and wore them out on the street.

During the first few weeks, we had built a bathhouse, and we were each given one quart of water to wash with every day. Just after the shift change, the line in front of the bathhouse would be hundreds of yards long. There were three rooms, and the water was heated in six big gasoline drums in the central room, scooped out in cans and handed through windows to the prisoners in the two washrooms. Each washroom had twelve wooden basins, most of which leaked. When the water ran out, they would dump snow in the drums, and if your turn came right afterward, your bath water would hardly be melted. On the other hand, if you were first in line after work, the water would be so hot you couldn't put your finger in it. The bathhouse itself was always freezing. Of course there was no soap, and after we washed, we had to put on the same filthy clothes. I began to think that the place had been erected purely for laughs. I hated to go in there. Undressing, we could see how skinny we had become.

No matter how careful I was, my felt boots would always get wet. Actually it didn't make much difference, since I had them on my feet for eighteen or twenty hours a day and they were getting very worn. I just hoped that they would last until the snow was gone. They barely did, and the last two weeks they had large holes in the sole. After the snow melted, I cut the bottoms off the boots and used the rest as a pillow. I didn't want to part with those boots; they had saved my feet.

Just as I was getting used to walking barefoot, one of the foremen from inside the mine suggested to the *atkatka* foreman of my shift that they could make galoshes for me if they took two pairs, cut them at the right place, and sewed them together with wire. They spoke to me about it, but I said that the officer in charge would never issue me two pairs of galoshes. The two foremen just laughed.

"The mine will issue them, because they need young, strong, willing workers. Anyway, what are two pairs of galoshes to the Soviet Union?"

Sure enough, the supply officer sent two pairs of galoshes to one of the local shoemakers, who made me a special pair. I was given some old canvas material to wrap my feet in, and considering everything, the galoshes didn't fit badly. However, it occurred to me that all this kindness was only so that I could work inside the mine.

For a week I worked on the wet level in Mine 89, but then I was inexplicably transferred to Mine 31. I thought it must be some bureaucratic mistake. In any case, I escaped an almost certain death from exhaustion and exposure. Later I heard that they had given up the wet level entirely, because it was impossible to get the quota of eight tons of coal out of every shift.

Life became reasonably simple. Mine 31 wasn't far from the camp, and I received a ration of a thousand grams, or about a third of a loaf of bread every day. In the mine I always filled my quota, and for this I was liked among the Russians; whenever they could, they gave me extra food, which they knew I needed badly and appreciated even more.

I was the youngest prisoner in the camp. Some of the other young prisoners had been arrested with a father or other relative; I was alone. Having seen a father take bread from his own son, I did not look to the older prisoners for support. They had all they could do to take care of themselves. Most had come from better homes with money—professionals, engineers, accountants, business owners—but none of that mattered now. All you had was whatever you could find in yourself, and for most adults that did not include an understanding or an ear for a 16-or 17-year-old who was not their child. There was one great exception, and he was a simple working man.

In the commotion at the train station I had seen this little guy, Georg Marzell, whose family was from my village, being loaded into the wagon behind the one I was in. His nickname was Getz. He was almost a foot shorter and twenty years older than me, a supervisor in a cable factory, and a father who had left five children behind. I knew him because his sister had worked for my father. They came from a large family, and their father was a farmer. Getz had six older brothers who were all giants. He was the youngest, and he had stayed small, but his spirit was gigantic.

Getz had a kind word for anyone who needed it. For us younger prisoners, in particular, he always had an encouraging word and a pat on the shoulder. As time went on a strong emotional bond developed between him and me. There were others who also relied on him. It was a magical force or warmth that he had. Getz couldn't help with the lack of food, the brutal work or the cold, but he helped to keep our spirits up.

Hardly any of the prisoners seemed to notice the coming of spring, for their strength was getting low and they only had enough energy to work and eat and rest. But still one could feel a change. The sun was getting warmer, and her warmth was so precious and necessary. Grass was coming out, and little flowers were opening up, and looking at them whenever I could steal ten or fifteen minutes to myself was like putting salve on an open wound. The spring brought up floods of memories from the past, which were all that I really possessed of my own. I clung to them, but at times when my feelings became too intense I would have to suppress my tears. I thought that indulging in sad memories was too great a luxury and would weaken me. During eight hours inside the mine I had to be alert. It was impossible to be a dreamer.

One day when our shift was over, I was thinking about my bread ration when the guard who marched us back to camp took me aside and led me to the foreman of the next shift. The foreman asked me if I wanted to earn an extra thousand grams of bread. Naturally I said yes, and he said that he was one loader short and needed a man badly on the *samaia zapadnaia lava,* which was the easternmost level. The guard broke in and told him that it was unnecessary to give me an extra ration of bread, since I had to do as I was told, anyway. But the foreman winked at me behind the guard's back and told me to see him at the end of the shift. The guard went off muttering, and I started back down into the mine. The prospect of working another eight hours didn't even bother me as I thought about the extra bread. Two thousand grams! Still, I would have liked some of it now.

The *samaia zapadnaia lava* was on the lowest level. When I got down there, one of the Russian girls pointed out the direction and said, "Vanya, you have a long walk ahead of you." I thanked her and set off down the tunnel. It was a wet level. I walked and walked and walked. Gradually I realized that I was all alone inside the earth. Water was dripping everywhere; each drop echoed as it hit the ground. As I thought about it, it became louder and louder. I stopped. I could hardly move for fear. The dancing shadows from my lamp…the dripping water…the old rotten braces…the stale moist smell…I was in hell. I was under the impression that I had walked for hours, but there was no sign of the *samaia zapadnaia lava.* How long could this level be?

The shadows kept getting larger and smaller, and the dripping water louder and more punctuated, like an insane infernal clock. I started walking again, but very slowly and cautiously, for I was afraid if I walked fast, my light would go out. The thought made me shudder. I walked even slower. I was losing all conception of time. Then I heard a faint, faint noise. It gave me a start at first, but nevertheless I increased my pace toward it. It sounded human. Soon I saw a gaping hole in the wall about five feet up. It was pitch black. Carefully I started climbing up the level. The ceiling was four and a half feet high, which was typical of the levels in Mine 31. I saw a faint light about fifty-five yards away. As I got closer I heard terrible, panting grunts, sometimes subdued, sometimes loud and desperate. I still couldn't see where they came from.

Finally, about twenty-three feet from the light, which was fastened to one of the braces, I saw an ageless blackened creature, working furiously with his long-handled pick, chopping under the coal as far as the pick would reach. Then with a crowbar he broke the coal down. He paused, and then he raised his head and hollered, *"Dobiciiiiii...* [more coal]." The sound echoed down the level. I saw his face; he had deep-set eyes, a long nose that had been broken several times, and a huge gray, bushy beard. His wrinkles were all filled with coal dust. He looked at me and then asked whether I was Vanya from the camp. I said yes. He crawled toward me and reached into the satchel that was hanging from his shoulder and took out a huge chunk of bread. He broke it in half and gave half to me. I was really surprised, for abuse and curses were what I had expected from this old man. Instead, he handed me bread.

I shoveled the coal until the chute was full and then pushed it down into the empty cars. At times Andryushka, the old man, would shovel while I was pushing the coal down. Together we filled our quota of eight cars without much trouble. Then we went out, leaving the cars there, and I waited by the *atkatka* platform for the foreman and collected my thousand grams of bread. I ate it on my way back to camp, and there I got another thousand grams. I had only three hours to sleep before I would have to get up for my regular shift, but I didn't mind, for it had become increasingly difficult to sleep in camp.

As it grew warmer, millions of cockroaches appeared. One of the men stayed up one night and told us that he had killed thirteen hundred of them. They were especially active after dark, so it was better to work the night shift and sleep during the day. During the warm weather we had permission to sleep outside within ten meters, or about eleven yards, of the barracks, but even outside, they crawled into your ears and nose as you slept, and if you squashed one it smelled terrible. Sometimes I was so tired that they could crawl anywhere they wanted to; I couldn't care less. Nevertheless, every day I got more and more determined: I had to escape.

Ever since the camp had gotten fairly well organized, the Russians had been showing propaganda films every week. The guards woke up the sleeping shifts, for everyone had to watch. The movies were shown in the first-aid barracks where rows and rows of benches were set up. I had seen such pictures in Romania. The only difference was that this time the Soviets were the saints, and the Germans were the foremost villains, worse even than the rest of the capitalists. After each film we had to shout enthusiastically and clap our hands as hard as we could. After the war ended, on the eighth of May, 1945, the enthusiasm of the more patriotic Russians doubled. Everywhere we heard: "We beat the German capitalist warmongers; now we'll beat the Americans."

One day Andryushka, whom I still saw at times, told me that he had heard rumors that the best workers among the prisoners would be moved to another camp. Thinking about it, I decided that it couldn't be any worse than our camp, so my only regret was losing the Russian friends I had made at the mine. I could talk with them already, and every day I learned a few more words.

The rumor turned out to be true. Five days later I was told, along with four other men from my shift, to stay behind when the others went to work, and a few hours later fifty men and twenty women from the camp were loaded into five trucks. Getz was also in my truck. They were large American transports with eight wheels in the back and two in front. In fact, practically the only trucks I had seen in Russia were American. The coal from the smaller mines was brought to the larger mines in trucks to be shipped from there by rail. This went on twenty-four hours a day, and if it rained a little the clayish ground became like glue. I doubt that an ordinary truck could have made it, but these American vehicles seemed indestructible. They growled, sputtered, and whined, but they got through. The few Russian trucks I had seen had only four wheels, and they were used to carry food and lumber. Sometimes they got stuck in the mud even when they were empty, and the American trucks would have to come and pull them out. Meanwhile the propaganda films continued to insist that the trucks and automobiles in America operated on wooden wheels, because there was no rubber left.

Chapter IV

THE RIDE TO the new camp was terribly bumpy. Somewhat reckless, too. Apparently we weren't as precious as a cargo of anthracite. The countryside was flat and barren except for a sunflower field now and then. There were very few trees, and those looked out of place and stunted. Scattered everywhere were mines of all sizes; their slag hills dotted the endless plain. We went through several small cities, with paved streets and solid-looking stone buildings. Outside the towns were railroad crossings. At one point we drove underneath a huge high-power electrical line. The entire coal mine area was supplied from this line. It was supposed to be very straight, and it went toward the Dnieper River and Dniepropetrovsk, the large city where we had stopped and gotten food on the way from Romania. This was a good thing to know, especially if one had ideas about escaping from the labor paradise.

Finally we arrived at an enclosure near the outskirts of a village. Inside, there was a single barracks building about fifty-five yards long.

The barbed-wire fence was only six feet high. We passed through the gate, and as soon as we got out, the trucks sped away. A smiling officer appeared, accompanied by several civilians dressed in soldier hats and carrying rifles. The officer asked who spoke Russian, and several of us raised our hands. He pointed to me and asked me my name, and then how old I was. I lied and said soon eighteen. He laughed, saying, "We will be needing young, strong boys like you at the mine." He picked a man around thirty who spoke Russian about as well as I did to be the official interpreter.

The officer explained to him that Mine 28, about a mile away, had just resumed operating. Before the war it had been the best producer in the entire Donbas region. During the German occupation, the mine had been under water, and it had only recently been pumped out. Soon it would be producing three hundred tons of coal a day. We had been sent here because each of us had acquired a reputation as a good worker in the other camp.

After the interpreter translated this for the rest of the prisoners, we were taken to the mine. The road sloped down a little, and we could see it in the distance as we started out. On the way we passed a field of sunflowers in bloom. What a beautiful rich yellow they were!

Behind the mine was a large square of wooden buildings surrounding a courtyard. The *stalovaya*, or mess hall, the supply shack, the mine headquarters, and the living quarters of some of the Russians were all located here. Although we had already been given our bread rations in the morning before we left the old camp, at the mess hall they gave us another ration as well as a midday soup. The mess hall was a large whitewashed room with long wooden tables and benches. One side was for the Russians and the other for prisoners. At the end of the room were two windows through which the food was passed from the kitchen. The soup was better and thicker than the soup we had been eating so far. The kitchen help, mostly female, laughed and kidded around. The cook was life itself. He was so big and fat he looked like a grinning moon. His name was Borisovich. He was a Georgian, not a Russian, and he was proud of this because Stalin was also a Georgian. He was a ladies' man, too. In the kitchen, which was his domain, he was always pinching his more attractive helpers on the behind.

After we had eaten, and the exclamations had died down about how much better the food was, we were taken to the supply shack. Before we left the other camp, they had taken away everything that had been issued to us there. An officer said in Russian, "Everyone will receive canvas pants, shirt, and galoshes." I was curious to see what would happen in my case, because I knew that they wouldn't have galoshes my size. My turn came, and I went in. The officer was sitting on a chair, and a Russian clerk behind a counter gave me a pair of pants and a shirt. They were brand new, made of a strong, canvas-like linen. The shirt fitted; the pants came to my ankles, because the waist was a little large. But after I had tried on about four pairs of galoshes, they told me to wait till everyone else was outfitted.

I stepped to the side. It was funny, I thought, that the pants and shirts were all snow white. These clean white clothes and the black coal...Why hadn't they issued black clothes, or some darker shade? I thought it was terrible for the black to invade the pure and innocent white. It wasn't only the coal that black represented to me. It was the suffering and misery all around me. The white would turn an ugly grey, and then an ugly black, and then holes would appear, and bigger holes, and if not somehow mended—death.

After everyone was fitted, I began trying on boots. The clerk cursed the size of my feet, damned the galoshes, and swore at the factory they were made in, as the officer laughed harder and harder. But by the time I had tried on the thirtieth pair, the clerk had exhausted the vocabulary of curses, and the officer was tired of laughing. They were both positive that galoshes my size were not made in the Soviet Union. The officer decided that since it was summer and I would be working outside, I could go barefoot.

From the supply shack the officer sent us with a guard to the *atkatka* platform. The *atkatka* was the flat top of a small hill about twenty-five feet high, and it was about thirty yards long and twenty-two yards wide. The entrance of the mine shaft was near one of the short edges. Behind the *atkatka* were the headquarters and other buildings, and on either side of it were the coal hill and the slag hill. The cars were pulled out of the mine three at a time by a cable as thick as a man's wrist that went around a wheel at the entrance and then up at a thirty-degree angle to a tower on the other side of the *atkatka*. This tower went up from the ground just beyond the *atkatka* hill; it was about twenty yards high and as large as a small house at the base. The cable went around a heavy wheel at the top of the tower and then down to the machine house ten yards behind.

When the cars got to the *atkatka* they were unhooked and the cable was transferred to empty cars on the other track waiting to go down. The full cars were then pushed by three *atkatchiki* onto the wooden platforms, where they were tipped over on their sides so that the coal fell onto the pile below.

The most important man on the *atkatka* was the *Nachal'nik Dvijeni*, whose name was Sirienko. *Dvijeni* means movement, and the

Nachal'nik Dvijeni or Foreman of Movement was in charge of everything besides the actual mining of the coal in the veins, which was under a different foreman on each level. The rail system and the cars, the tunnels, the main shaft, and everything outside the mine were under Sirienko's jurisdiction. I met him at the *atkatka* platform. He was a small, wiry man about fifty years old; his long face was weather-beaten into an endless maze of wrinkles, and his deep-set eyes moved constantly. In spite of his size, he carried an air of authority. He looked at my feet and then at my face and asked me how old I was. I told him, and then he asked me whether I knew anything about *atkatkas*. I said I had worked on several of them before, and that what I didn't know, I could learn. He winked at me. "One of my supervisors is a pretty girl named Marusya. You start on her shift tomorrow morning.

"And watch your feet," he called after me.

I was surprised. A Russian, and one who was obviously somebody just by the way his name was uttered, had told me to be careful of my feet because I could get hurt. The guards slapped me on the shoulder and laughed and made jokes. Altogether the experiences of the day seemed too good to be true. Compared to the other camp, this one was almost like being free.

After everyone had been assigned to different shifts and levels, we went back to camp.

The Prisoners at Mine 28

We did not have to march in single file, but were allowed to walk in groups. That also was something new. At the barracks there were only seventy of us, and we weren't crowded at all. Nevertheless, before I went to sleep, the idea of escaping went through my head as it did every night. This time I thought that if only I knew how long we were going to be kept in Russia, I might be able to just wait it out. After all, the war was over, although Russia would probably continue to occupy Romania for a number of years. But what I dreaded was the winter. I would have to make up my mind soon whether I was going to escape or try to survive another winter. These thoughts kept me from sleeping well that night. But the next day I felt good. At work I wanted to show them what I knew.

Marusya, the supervisor on the *atkatka*, introduced me to several Russian girls working on my shift, and we got along very well. They flirted a little with me, and two girls I met that day would remain friendly with me throughout my stay at Mine 28. One's name was Nina, and the other was Lisa. Nina gave me a good slice of bread from her satchel at lunch. Her job was counting the tons of coal being pulled out of the mine. The norm for our mine was three hundred tons of coal in twenty-four hours. That was a little too high, but norms were always set a little high to keep the workers trying. I worked with Lisa unloading the first wagon.

The *kanat* (cable) pulled three wagons at a time out of the mine, all hooked together. Behind the *atkatka* was a large shack where a huge winch, the *libyotka*, pulled the cable out of the earth with three full wagons and let it down the shaft again with the empty ones. The *libyotka* made a wretched sound. The winch operator applied the brakes as he let the wagons slide back into the mouth of the earth. And it made such a sad whining noise, to my imagination it sounded as if all the sorrow the people here had lived through was being screamed to the skies. I could hear it at night as I lay awake in the barracks, a mile away. The howling wind mixed with the whining of the *libyotka* is a sound I will remember as long as I breathe.

The first day after work the guard said that I could walk back to camp alone. It was like a dream. It was so beautiful to be able to walk by myself and take my time. I stopped to pick a sunflower and suck on the tiny seeds.

Back at camp another friendly guard told me I could go and wash myself in a small creek about half a mile away. This creek supplied drinking water for several of the nearby villages. I followed the guard's

directions and found a small stream about two yards wide and as much
as forty inches deep in some places. There were small trees and bushes
by the water, and I walked along the stream until I found a nice spot
under some bushes. After I had rested a while, I undressed and washed
myself, and then I sat down in the knee-deep water. The sun felt so
warm. I splashed and drank myself full of the clear, cold water. After
drying out in the sun, I put my pants and shirt back on. They were still
clean. I lay down in the shade of the bushes. Being alone was a kind of
nourishment. After a while I reluctantly decided to go back to camp,
because I didn't want to spoil this privilege by staying away too long.

When I returned to the barracks, the officer was telling a group of
prisoners that we would all be allowed to go to the creek to wash ourselves until they built a bathhouse at the mine. I was a bit disappointed.
I decided that I would have to go farther down the creek. The next day
I started to explore. The creek wound industriously toward the south. I
never did find out what river it emptied into. Probably the Don. The
course of the creek could be followed from the *atkatka* and from the top
of the *poroda* hill because of the trees and bushes near the water.

Poroda was the stones and slate and other useless slag taken out of
the mine. When a carload came out, it was hooked to a cable that was
pulled by a small winch at the top of the large flat hill of slag. This hill
was about two stories high and as large as a city block. A new level was
being blasted, and as result the mine was now producing between thirty and eighty carloads of *poroda* every day. Since the slag was not taken
away, the hill grew and grew.

Before long I found myself a steady *porodchik*. It took three strong
men to tip over a car of *poroda* and then shovel it out. *Poroda* was about
three times as heavy as coal, and much harder to handle; many of the

workers on the *atkatka* who handled coal cars were women, but only men could handle *poroda*. Every time we finished a carload, we would rest and talk. In general, it was much less noisy and nerve-racking than working on the *atkatka,* where a group of three cars of coal came up every twenty minutes or so; as soon as they arrived, there was a constant pressure to empty them so that the cars could be sent back down for more coal.

I became a favorite of Sirienko's because I applied myself and also, I think, because being a little man, he liked big men. When I was needed, I was always there. After a few weeks he knew he could depend on me.

Sometimes when the *poroda* load was light, I would help with the heavy 100-pound hook that was used to raise and lower the train. On one such day the *Golovoi*, who was the head of the whole mine, stood around the *atkatka* watching us for about six hours. As he left for his office, he told me to report to him after the shift was over. He called me Vanya. It was a big thing. He called very few Russians by their first names, and he never spoke to prisoners at all.

The *Golovoi's* office was in the headquarters building which was next to the mess hall. I went in and the *Golovoi* told his secretary to give me one coupon for two extra meals and one for twenty feet of heavy material for clothes. He said it was for the speed and skill with which I changed the hook. Within a few hours, everybody knew about it. I didn't know what to do with the material, so eventually I sold it to a foreman for 400 rubles, or about a hundred dollars.

Chapter V

I LOOKED FORWARD to the afternoons, when I could walk to the creek and spend an hour or two alone under a little willow tree I had found, listening to the birds and the flowing of the water. It was my own private place, and here I built up my reserves. One day at the creek I met an old Russian who had come for water. He was carrying a pail on each end of a long board balanced on his shoulders. It was easier than carrying the pails by hand; sometimes water had to be carried as far as two or three miles on foot. This old Russian had a very kind face and eyes. His name was Nikolai and he told me that he was a kind of village elder or official. Then he said:

"I would like to have you come to my house for dinner sometime."

"Well," I began, "it may be difficult, because the guards..."

"Nonsense," he interrupted. "The sergeant of the guards lives near my house. I know him well, and I'm sure I can arrange it with him. Don't worry."

We talked for some time. I learned that most of the Russians who worked at Mine 28 lived in his village, which was called Takinya and was about a mile away. Finally it was time to go. Nikolai said he would talk to the sergeant of the guards and meet me again at the creek the next afternoon. As I walked slowly back to the camp I felt warm, thinking about the friendly old man. I looked forward to eating a regular meal and to visiting a Russian home. I was very curious to see how these people lived.

The time went by slowly. At work it was a little better, since I was busy, but I didn't really relax until I was on my way back to the creek the next day. Nikolai was waiting for me and greeted me with a big "Hello, Vanya."

He told me, "You can come to dinner tomorrow. I spoke to the sergeant, and he said that it would be all right as long as you don't stay away more than eight hours."

I felt grateful and embarrassed. "Nikolai, can I help you with anything at home? Perhaps I can help with the chores around the house that might be too hard for an old man." At this he threw his head back and gave a hearty laugh. Then he said, "No, no. But if something hard comes up and I need some help, I'd be glad to ask you."

Then he held my arm, and I felt that he was touched by my gesture. It embarrassed me all the more.

Back in camp I found a group of fifty German girls, newly arrived from East Prussia. Most of them were between twenty and thirty years old. I had learned German in school during the German occupation of Romania, and I talked with them a bit. They seemed to have a lot of spirit, considering that they had been living under the Hitler regime for years. I knew what would happen to all this spirit and bounce after a few months of hard work.

The next day some of the new girls were assigned to the mine and some to the *atkatka*. There were four of them on our shift. I didn't pay too much attention to them, though, because my thoughts were occupied by my coming visit to Nikolai's house and the meal I would eat. Time dragged, but the whistle finally blew one…then two…then three o'clock. I gulped down my ration of cabbage soup and kasha at the mess hall and walked back to camp as fast as I could. When I got there, the sergeant of the guards told me not to worry about the rest of the afternoon, as long as I was back by nine o'clock. I went directly to the creek to meet Nikolai. He was there waiting for me, and I washed myself while he stood by watching. I was embarrassed because I was so skinny. When I finished, he filled his two pails with water and we started off. I offered to carry the pails.

"No, Vanya, it will be faster if I carry them myself. It takes some practice to learn how to balance them. Some other time you can try it."

On the way to the house Nikolai told me that he had been a miner all his life until about eight years before, when he had had a bad accident and was unable to continue working. Then the war had started. "Ah, Vanya," he sighed, "the war is a terrible thing. Everyone—the whole world suffered because of men like Hitler." He stopped and rolled a cigarette, using a piece of *Pravda* newspaper. Then he asked me about my home. "Are your mother and father living? Do they know you are here in the coal mine?" I replied that my parents were alive, but they didn't know where I was. He shook his head and said, "Oh, misery."

We came to a small village of about fifty houses. They were made of clay, and most of them were whitewashed. Nikolai stopped at the fifth house on the main street. In front of it was a small vegetable garden. A young woman about thirty years old appeared in the doorway. Nikolai introduced us. "This is Natasha, my wife. Natasha, this is Vanya." I must have blushed, because she laughed. "You must be very young, Vanya," she teased. We entered the house and went into a large room with white walls and a scrubbed wooden floor. In the middle of it there was a heavy oak table with four strong wooden chairs around it, and against one of the walls was a huge stove made out of clay, with a cast-iron top which had rings so it could be lifted off with a hook. There were three big pots on the stove. Nikolai showed me their bedroom. It was about half the size of the other room and was furnished with a rough oak chest and a homemade double bed. Everything was clean and tidy. Natasha told us to sit down and eat. We ate out of huge wooden bowls. She served us a rich borscht, which is a cabbage soup with huge chunks of pork and beef in it. After that we had baked beans. I ate two full plates of the delicious borscht, and when I had finished my first plate of beans, I looked at Natasha and she laughed and emptied the rest of the pot in my plate. "You must be very hungry," she said, "being so young and a prisoner."

For dessert we had cornmeal cakes with honey on them. Honey was very hard to get on the market. Nikolai explained that he had some bees behind the house in the garden and told me to eat as much as I wanted. Then Natasha brought a large clay bowl full of milk and three cups to dip into it. Soon there was no more milk left. I was really full. I thanked them over and over, and told them several times that I hadn't eaten so well since I had left home. Natasha gave me a handful of roasted sunflower seeds and bade me goodbye, saying that she had to go to her neighbor's for a while. She went out. I asked Nikolai if I could help him in any way in return. I felt that the only way I could show him my appreciation was by doing some physical labor for him.

Finally he said, "As a matter of fact, Vanya, do you think there is anyone in the camp who has a watch to sell? I want to get one for Natasha, and it's impossible to buy one. I know that the officers usually manage to requisition all such luxuries, but if you can find someone who had hidden one away I will pay fifteen cups of honey for it."

I'll do my best to find one," I said, "and as soon as I do, I'll tell the sergeant of the guards to tell you. Whoever has the watch can bargain with you about the price."

Nikolai said not to tell the sergeant about it, because we could both get into serious trouble. We decided to meet every Friday by the creek to remain in contact with each other. After two or three weeks he would invite me again for dinner.

On the way back to camp I thought a little about the age difference between the Russian couple. Nikolai was around fifty and gray-haired, an old man worn down by hard labor. His wife was between twenty-five and thirty, and very good-looking. It was hard to understand. Together they looked like father and daughter. Anyhow, I had to find someone with a watch to sell. I figured that the most likely place to discover one would be among the new arrivals from East Prussia. The next morning I would ask one of the German girls on our shift. If someone did have a watch, it wouldn't be hard to persuade her to sell it, because fifteen cups of honey was an irresistible luxury. Besides, if she didn't sell it, it would probably end up on the wrist of one of the officers or interpreters.

As I walked through the gate, the sergeant asked if everything had been all right. My cheerful yes seemed to please him. The next morning I casually questioned some of the prisoners about a watch. The universal reply was that no one knew of anyone with anything, but would ask someone else for me. I had expected this, so I wasn't discouraged.

The next day at work I was resting between cars of *poroda* and watching the activity on the *atkatka* platform when I saw one of the German girls straining with all her might to put an empty car back on the rails. The two front wheels were off, and she was just barely strong enough to keep the car from slipping any farther. She was a very slight girl, and I was amazed at the effort she was making. I rushed down and put the car back on the rails for her. She turned, surprised at the unexpected help, and I was taken aback by her pretty oval face and deep-blue eyes. Her name was Erika. We talked and afterwards I found myself thinking about her.

A few days later she told me she had found someone who had a watch and who was interested in the fifteen cups of honey. I was overjoyed. Privately I hadn't really believed that anyone still had a watch. I couldn't wait to tell Nikolai the good news. The next day was Friday, and I went rushing down to the creek. I had to wait about an hour before he came. He was very pleased and told me to bring the girl on Saturday and he would bring the honey.

That evening in camp I told Erika the plan. She said that the other girl was in another shift and so she would ask her to give us the watch and we could bring back the honey. The next morning on the way to work, she told me that she had the watch hidden inside her blouse. After work we went together to the creek. Nikolai was waiting with a big can of honey about half the size of a pail. He looked at the watch, which Erika had carefully wrapped in a handkerchief. It was a small, round lady's watch with a gold-plated frame. We showed him how to wind it and adjust the time. He said he liked it and asked whether the price was right. I translated, and Erika nodded yes. He gave her the can of honey. He asked me please to return the can because he needed it on his trips to the bazaar. Then he pulled a cloth package from the pocket of his coat and gave it to me. It was from Natasha. I carefully unfolded the cloth and found four beautiful brown pieces of cornmeal cake. I gave two to Erika and began to eat my two. Nikolai laughed and asked me if I liked Erika. I blushed and nodded, saying I had only known her for a little while, though. He laughed again. "You should marry her." Without looking at him I said that we were prisoners and lived in a camp. He became suddenly solemn and shrugged helplessly with his shoulders and hands. "I know, Vanya, but what can I do?" A little while later he left, inviting me for dinner again the following Friday.

I showed Erika my special spot by the creek. Then I took my shirt off and started to wash myself. Erika disappeared farther down the creek, and after a while she came back washed. She thanked me for the two pieces of cake. Gradually our conversation drifted to our homes. She lived in a suburb of Koenigsberg, the capital of East Prussia. She had lost her father and four brothers in the war, being left alone with her mother, who was old and sick, and four younger children. They lived on a small pension, and Erika took care of the children. Then one day the Russians had come to her house and taken her.

We talked for several hours. She was surprised by my age, and she was impressed by the way I handled myself with the Russians and by my knowledge of German. Finally I decided we'd better go back to camp. I carried the honey for her; we spoke very little on the way back. I knew that she liked me, and that it was up to me to encourage this relationship, but I couldn't. I would have my hands full taking care of myself. That day at the creek was as far as I allowed myself to get involved with Erika.

Chapter VI

DURING SOME SHIFTS a lot of *poroda* came out of the mine, and during others we handled only a few cars full. It took three of us about forty minutes to tip over a car and shovel out the heavy, clumsy slag. There was no regularity in its production, and sometimes five or six cars would come out at once; it would take several hours to unload them, and the cars, which were needed in the mine, would be tied up. If more cars came up, workers would be taken off the *atkatka* to help unload them. Sometimes almost the whole *atkatka* shift would be up on the slag hill, sweating and cursing, while Sirienko stood by and fumed.

Several times while I was working, Sirienko came up to watch. His face was pensive, and he had a pencil and a piece of paper on which he scribbled notes. Finally one of the Russians I worked with asked him what it was all about. Sirienko's face wrinkled into a smile. He explained that it took too much time to unload a wagon of *poroda*. He was going to build a fifty-foot tower on top of the *poroda* hill near the edge, with rails leading up to the top of the tower on scaffolding. A small machine house would be built next to the large one and the cable would run up to the tower, around a wheel, and back down the rails to the *poroda* car. When the car reached the top, it would simply be tipped over and the slag would fall out. He had ordered the blacksmith to construct a special car that could be emptied without the wheels leaving the rails; only the bed of the car was to move. Finally, he had designed a chute to be built at the edge of the *atkatka*, so that the *poroda* cars coming out of the mine could be tipped over into the chute and the slag would fall into the special car, which would then take it up to the top of the tower. It was a simple system, but Sirienko said that it would cut our time and work to a quarter of what it was.

Two days later, five Russian carpenters started building the tower and the scaffolding for the rails out of heavy twelve-inch-square beams. They worked at it every day during the 7 A.M. to 3 P.M. shift. Sirienko worked beside them, driving them, shouting commands and directions. Only twelve days later everything was finished and ready for a trial run.

Sirienko had invited the *Golovoi* and some of the more important supervisors to watch the operation. The new car was still a little stiff, for although it was well oiled, it wasn't a factory product. It was pushed under the chute and the cable was hooked to it. A car full of *poroda* was dumped into the chute from the *atkatka,* and it rolled right down into the new car. One of the two Russians who were to tip the car over at the top stepped onto the base of the car in front and gave a signal to the operator in the little window of the small machine house. The other Russian was afraid to ride and said he would walk up behind the car. The cable grew taut and the whole structure groaned a little. The car started to move slowly up at a forty-five-degree angle, first on the side of the slag hill, and then on the scaffolding, which started where the *poroda* hill leveled off. As the car got near the top of the tower, the Russian raised his arm, giving the signal to stop. The other Russian was clambering up the ties like a monkey. When he got to the top, they removed the safety hook from the car. Standing on the ties on the side, they pushed the body of the car up, but they couldn't get it over the dead point. They tried five or six times without success. The tower was swaying visibly. The *Golovoi* and the foreman shook their heads. Sirienko shouted, "Rock it back and forth." They rocked it a few times gingerly and every time they did, the whole construction creaked and swayed. Sirienko shook his fist at them and cursed. Finally they got up enough nerve to rock it strongly, and after a dozen times back and forth the car tipped over. The *poroda* thundered down.

The empty car returned with the two Russians in it. As soon as they got out, they started complaining bitterly to Sirienko about how difficult it was to get the car over the dead point. While everyone was talking and gesticulating excitedly I went over to the car and took at look at it. I removed the safety hook and tried to tip it over, and it moved quite easily. Of course it was empty, but even so I decided that it couldn't have been all that heavy when it was full. I went back to the group and asked Sirienko whether I could try it out once. Everyone looked at me as if I were crazy, but Sirienko said, "Go ahead, try it, Vanya."

Another load of *poroda* was dumped into the car. I stepped onto the front of it and signaled the winch operator, and soon I was on my way up. I was a bit scared, but it was a nice feeling to be pulled higher and higher. I could look over the whole area. At the top I signaled the winch operator to stop. There was room enough on the ties to stand comfortably. I removed the safety hook, rocked the car once, and then gave it a solid push, and it tipped over. I realized suddenly that it was easy for me simply because I was six feet two inches tall, so that I had plenty of leverage at the point where a strong push was needed. A shorter man would have to use twice as much strength. It seemed as if the car had been built especially for me.

The two Russians who had made the first trip were both built like bears, but neither of them was over five feet eight inches tall. When I got back down they were looking at me open-mouthed, and Sirienko was cursing at them, "You see? One prisoner does better than two Turks!" Turning to me, he said, "Very fine. You will be my best *porodchik.*"

I felt proud, and a little sorry for the two Russians. It wasn't their fault that they weren't as tall as I. Still, they were pretty stupid not to realize that it was just a matter of height. In any case, now I was assured of a fairly easy job. The beauty of it was that everyone thought it was a very hard job, and that I must be a Hercules to perform it.

I was alone on my shift, while each of the other shifts had two men. I liked it; there was no one to tell me what to do or how to do it. By myself I managed better than either of the two other shifts. Sirienko had arranged for me to get a ration of a thousand grams of bread a day, which was as much as the workers inside the mine got; the normal ration for workers on the *atkatka* and the *poroda* hill was seven hundred grams.

There was an enormous difference between working inside the mine and working outside. I hadn't been in Mine 28, but I knew it couldn't be much different from the others. The stories the prisoners brought back to camp in the evenings were essentially the same. From the tower I could see one shift going into the mine fairly clean, and fifteen minutes later the previous shift would more or less crawl out of that dark, forbidding hole, their faces black, dead tired....Unlike the other mines, Mine 28 had a separate entrance for the workers. There were ladders, in ten sections of forty meters or about forty-four yards each, which went straight down from a small shack near the mess hall; the ladders only went as far as the first level, and from there on, the workers had to go through abandoned levels full of rats and excrement. It was very hard to climb those ladders after eight hours of hard work. Even as they were leaving, the prisoners were driven, this time by impatient and well-fed young Russian workers who had plenty of stamina left and wanted to get home fast. As the prisoners emerged from the mine, a guard stood by and counted them.

The tower was the highest point in the whole area. At the top I could feel the sun shining and breathe in the fresh, clean air and watch the work at the mine like a movie. The *atkatka* looked like an anthill. In the morning, after the bustle of shift change was over and the night shift had gone home, the activity on the platform would become more monotonous and regular as the sun got stronger and dried the last dew from the ground. Sometimes I would have only fifteen or twenty cars of slag to unload during the entire shift, which totaled no more than an hour's work. Perched between the sky and the ground, I would watch the birds fly. I longed to have wings and be free.

Another shipment of about a hundred prisoners arrived. They were put into an old barracks a few hundred yards away from the camp. During the German occupation, horses had been kept in it. On my day off I was assigned to one of the details that put up a barbed-wire fence around the new camp. Now the total number of prisoners was about five hundred. This last bunch seemed in poor physical condition, but nothing about them bothered me very much because I had a job that made me feel good and clean.

Gradually my reputation grew, as it became known to the Russians that I was handling the *poroda* alone during my shift, whereas in each of the other shifts it was handled by two men. As I made friends among the Russians I was often given extra bread rations, sometimes as much as five hundred or a thousand grams. My work record also became known to the captain of the camp and to the guards, and I became something of a privileged prisoner.

Some of the other prisoners were jealous of my status and resented my friendliness with the Russians, but not Getz. When something good happened I could always look forward to coming back to the barracks and telling him; his face would light up. The little guy had the heart of a lion.

About two weeks later, Sirienko invited me to his house for dinner. I was very pleased, but I reminded him that I was a prisoner and subject to camp rules. He merely laughed and said he would speak to the captain and everything would be arranged. Two days later he passed by the *atkatka* to tell me that I could go with him to his house that afternoon.

After work I waited around the *atkatka* for him. At four o'clock I finally spotted him coming from the direction of the officers' headquarters. He was weaving a little, and as he approached he yelled, "How are you, Vanyushka? Come on, let's go and eat."

We started on our way. He lived in a small settlement about a mile from the mine, past our camp. It was similar to the village where Nikolai lived, but the houses were slightly larger and in better condition. I learned later that several of the important foremen from the mine lived here. Sirienko's house was twice as big as Nikolai's. A neat white fence surrounded it. Sirienko's wife met us. She was an older, cranky woman who acted like a shrew. As soon as we had exchanged how-do-you-do's she started complaining about Sirienko's drunkenness and his being late "as usual." He turned to me and laughingly said, "She's always like that. Ignore her." He told her to feed us.

We went through the kitchen into a large living room with a heavy oak dining table in the middle with chairs around it. In one corner was a couch, and in front of it was a low table. Some papers and a few books were on the table. When we came in, everything was neat and clean, but Sirienko immediately started strewing things around like a bear. He went into another room on the side and brought out a bottle of vodka and two tall glasses. He started pouring a glass for me, and I said that I didn't drink. "You will now," he said. "Tell me when to stop." I stopped him after he had poured two fingers' worth, but he ignored me and filled the glass half full. I took a small gulp, and it burned my throat like acid; I coughed for a full minute. Sirienko laughed until tears came out of his eyes, and his wife cursed under her breath.

The meal began with a steaming hot, rich borscht. Sirienko had only half a plate. He told me to forget about him and eat as much as I could. After the soup there was a delicious kasha with hunks of sheep meat in it. I ate and ate. I was still eating when Sirienko fell asleep on the table. His wife just kept serving me more food without saying a word. For dessert she gave me a bowl of milk and cornmeal cakes. When the bowl was empty, she filled it up again from a large jug. Then Sirienko woke up and asked me whether I had eaten enough. I said I had eaten excellently, and I thanked him, but he brushed my gratitude away with a gesture. "Go back to camp now, Vanya, and I'll see you in the morning."

I thanked his wife. To my surprise she told me to come back again. Maybe she enjoyed feeding someone who really ate. As I walked back to camp, I couldn't help wondering what was wrong between Sirienko and his wife. He was such a lively, easygoing guy, and she was so melancholy and disagreeable, and I could see that they didn't get along very well. I also knew that Sirienko didn't spend too much time at home, but preferred to wander around the mine, from the *atkatka* to the offices, or to the lumber places behind the *atkatka,* or even from level to level inside the mine. This was partly necessary, because he was in charge of all movement on rails, but I was sure that some of his wandering was done for want of something else to do.

Chapter VII

A DAY OR so later, Sirienko told me to come to work a little early the
next day so that we could talk. He seemed anxious and pensive, and I
wondered what he had on his mind. Maybe he had been criticized for
giving me a daily ration of a thousand grams of bread. But only the
Golovoi could criticize him, and even with the *Golovoi,* Sirienko usually
got his way. It was well known that there was no one who could replace
him. No one knew as much as he did about coal mines. Still, there was
a law that only workers inside the mine were allowed to receive a thousand grams of bread. I was working outside, and I wasn't even a Russian.
Maybe that was it.

The next day I got permission from the officer of the barracks to go
to work early. I found Sirienko waiting for me at the *atkatka.* He came
right to the point. He said that he wanted to get me out of the camp. To
do this I would have to marry a Russian girl. He would find me a place
to live, and I would continue to work for him. Eventually I could

become a Russian citizen, and I could work my way up to foreman. That wasn't all. He said he would help me with clothes and food. As it was now, it was difficult, because a number of people had already complained about my getting extra bread.

I was stunned. It was an unbelievable offer. The first thing I could think of to say was that I didn't think it would be possible, because I was under military jurisdiction. As far as I knew, the mine officials had nothing to do with the prisoners, beyond the fact that the officer in charge of the camp had to supply three shifts of workers every day. But Sirienko laughed at my doubts. "Vanya, I'll talk to your captain right in front of you. Also I know someone in the party to whom I can speak. I know I can arrange it."

This needed a lot of thought. I told him I had to think it over for a few days. He said of course, but I should let him know my decision as soon as possible. Just as he said this, the captain passed us. Sirienko called him and he came over. Again Sirienko came right to the point. He explained that he wanted to get me out of the camp, and asked the captain what steps he would have to take if I decided to marry a Russian. The captain looked very surprised. He kept talking and saying that Sirienko was the *Nachal'nik Dvijeni* and that he knew that I was the only one who could work the tower on top of the *poroda* hill alone. He advised Sirienko not to forget that I was a prisoner and under military supervision. Then he mentioned that Romania had fought on the German side against the Soviet Union for three years.

At this last remark, Sirienko got mad and told him that first of all I was only seventeen, and secondly I was the best worker on the *atkatka*. If I was willing to marry a Russian girl, he would see to it that everything was arranged. At this point in the argument I had to leave, because my shift had started. I could hear Nina calling me to unload a wagon of *poroda*.

I went to work feeling uneasy about the argument which I felt I had caused between Sirienko and the captain. I turned the offer over and over in my mind, looking at it from all sides. I didn't like it, although I was fairly sure that Sirienko would be able to manage it. Marrying one of the Russian girls would bring me some relief, but what kind of a future could I look forward to, working on the *atkatka* in Mine 28? Eventually I could become one of Sirienko's foremen, and perhaps in time I could replace Sirienko himself. But a shudder went through me when I thought of the kind of life I would be leading if I agreed. After two or three years they might send the rest of the prisoners home, and how would I feel then, knowing that they were returning to their families while I remained in this damned mine forever?

No! No! No! It just wasn't for me. But how could I turn down Sirienko without hurting his feelings? I turned the problem around and around in my mind for the next three days. I thought about it at work. I dreamed about it in my few sleeping hours. After considerable agitation I was exactly where I had started. If only I could figure out some way to tell him without making him angry!

The captain had already mentioned something about Sirienko's proposal to our interpreter. His manner indicated a new respect. I had been a special prisoner ever since I had started working on the *poroda* tower; no one ever bothered me with details except on my day off, and I still was allowed to walk home from work alone. But what would happen if Sirienko didn't stand behind me any more? I was fairly sure of only one thing: They wouldn't take me off the *poroda* tower. But I would probably lose my privileges. The extra food I got and the few moments of solitude I had were what kept me alive.

I thought that Sirienko probably had Nina in mind for me. We worked well together at the mine, and she was the feminine, domestic type. While most of the girls swore like men when they were mad, Nina never even raised her voice. She was a quiet person, perhaps a little too introverted. Her clear blue eyes were set in a perfectly oval face.

Once Nina's mother had been on some business outside her village, and she had passed by the mine to chat. Nina had introduced me to her, and I found her a nice old woman, a typical mother. Her husband and son had been killed in the war, and now she lived alone with Nina. They owned a cow and three goats. If a family had four such animals in this region, they were considered wealthy. While we were talking, Nina and her mother had invited me to their house for dinner, and since then Nina had repeated the invitation several times. The only problem was that their village was about eight miles away, and I would get in trouble if I left the camp for that long.

I thought of the trip Nina had in store for her, going and coming from the mine in the long, long winter evenings, with the deep snow. I wondered how many hours it would take her to walk the eight miles in a snowstorm. If she worked the night shift, and started work at 11 P.M., she would probably have to leave around 8 P.M.

And what did Nina and her mother do at home when it got dark at 3:30 in the afternoon? They probably sat together in the house drinking tea, talking or knitting, or else they slept. One would have to escape into something. Sleep, I imagine, was the best for them. But how would I fit into such a life? Crowding around the stove, with the cow and the goats on one side and the two women and myself on the other? What a breeding place for melancholy!

In not one of the houses I had visited had I seen more than five or six books. Sirienko had a few works of Tolstoy, Dostoyevsky, and Gogol lying around among scattered newspapers, but the rest of the homes had no books of any sort, outside of the Bible, which I had seen at Nikolai and Natasha's place. Nikolai was using the thin pages for cigarette paper against the feeble protests of Natasha, who declared it was a sin. But the urge to smoke was greater than the urge not to sin, so their Bible was dying page by page, until soon there would be nothing left but the cover.

I was a prisoner, but I didn't expect to be one for the rest of my life. I hadn't committed any crime, except for being born in a different country, a country that had been in a stupid war with Russia. Now Romania was on the Allied side. Could I outlast the days, weeks, perhaps years, until they sent the prisoners home again? Or should I choose the kind of life Nina was leading? My background was so different. Ninety percent of the men in the Donbas were coal miners. All the young men had to serve in the army, and if they chose an army career, fine. If not, back home they went and into the coal mines. At least they had been born in the Donbas, and it was practically all they knew.

I still had to give Sirienko an answer. I couldn't think of a way to word my answer so that he could understand why I couldn't accept his offer. It would mean giving up everything, including a chance of returning home. Fortunately he didn't press me. I saw him the next day, and the day after, and several days after that. He greeted me as he always had, and he seemed to have forgotten the conversation he had had with me.

At this time the Russian citizens who had been put in forced labor camps by the Germans during the war were returning home. During the week, Sirienko's two daughters came back from Prussia, where they had worked in a factory for the past two years. Everyone was talking about it. For a day or so, Sirienko wasn't seen. I thought that his daughters' return might take his mind off me, at least for the time being. And perhaps his happiness at seeing his family together again would make it easier for him to understand that I too had a family, and that they would be equally glad to see me after such a long absence. Well, I was wrong.

The next day at work, as I was coming down from the tower with an empty car, I spotted Sirienko with several other Russians, all drunk as lords, staggering toward the *atkatka*. Sirienko saw me and raised his fist at me and shook it, but I mistook it for a wave. When I got down, they were all roaring, and Sirienko shouted for me to come over. As I approached, he was cursing so violently that I thought something had happened to him. Then he picked up a piece of *poroda* the size of a fist and threw it at me as he cursed me, my mother, and everything else he could think of. His aim was bad because of the liquor, and I ducked the rock easily. I thought he had gone mad. The other Russians tried to quiet him down. "Not him, not him. That's your *porodchik*, Vanya."

"Don't worry," I shouted. "I don't want to stay here and work for you and marry a Russian girl. I want to go home, like your daughters came home!"

I didn't know whether he had heard me or not, but the moment I had let my feelings out, I felt much better. The offer which Sirienko had left with me for the last week had depressed me. Now it was decided.

That night I lay awake for a long time. I was sad because my friendship with Sirienko seemed to have come to an end. Then I started thinking about my situation. It was early fall. The windy days had become less and less comfortable on the *poroda* hill. Not that it was unbearable, but the thought of working on that tower during the winter with my thin jacket and shirt, being blown around by the strong eastern wind, had increased my depression. As each day passed, winter was a day closer. Nothing could postpone it, neither prayer nor command. Working on the tower would be bearable only if one had adequate clothing and meals. I began to wonder if it wouldn't be better to try to get into the mine. It was the only way to escape the merciless, cruel cold and the whistling, singing winds on top of the tower.

During the past two months I had spoken a few times to Sirienko about the inside of the mine, asking him about the conditions and about his function in it. It was during these talks that I discovered how much he knew about mining. I had noticed also that the foremen from the various levels frequently came to Sirienko to discuss safety conditions.

The ground talks a language that is known to few. Sirienko had been in several cave-ins but he had always escaped, thanks to his uncanny feeling for the shifting earth. The ground growls, aches and trembles, and at times there is a deathlike quiet, interrupted only by an occasional groan from an overloaded brace. There wasn't a thing inside the mine that Sirienko didn't know. Once when he and one of the foremen were discussing the mine, Sirienko went off for a few minutes, and I asked the foreman whether the *Golovoi* knew more about the inside of the mine than Sirienko. He just laughed and said, "No one knows more about this mine or any other mine, inside or outside, than Sirienko."

He also said that the *Golovoi* hated Sirienko because he was often drunk and he played around a lot. But his knowledge was essential, and it was well known that he was a very wise man.

The foreman had warned me not to get transferred into the mine. It took years of experience to learn how to observe the ground's reactions so that you knew how to avoid trouble. He also told me that the mine was treacherous and could rarely be trusted.

What was I to do? Sirienko was mad at me now. My chances of getting additional clothing to wear during the winter were practically gone. But when I thought of the treacherous black mine it was equally depressing. Finally I decided to leave things as they were for a while. So far, I had managed fairly well, considering everything.

An unusual thing occurred at about this time. Apparently the prisoners were supposed to be paid like everyone else. Of course, we had never heard about this, but several of the foremen from inside the mine had complained about it. The result was that starting the first of the month, we were to receive salaries like the Russians. That meant that we would have the privilege of paying the camp administration for our rations. We could do as we pleased with the rest. It sounded fine, but what would happen to the sick, and to the prisoners who had managed to get steady jobs doing camp details?

I should have gotten two salaries, because each of the other shifts had two men doing my job. The highest salary for an *atkatka* worker was three hundred and fifty rubles a month. I knew I could get that. It was the average salary for a worker inside the mine. In the levels one was paid according to one's production.

Later on, they worked it out so that everyone who received a salary had to pay a certain amount to the camp administration for his rations. If the salary exceeded one hundred rubles a month, one had to pay more. The more you received, the more you paid. It was a great system. Also, the interpreters started fining people for various minor misdemeanors, and this money helped pay for the sick.

Nevertheless, I felt good about the change. I knew that I would be able to save some money to buy myself some winter clothing. The first thing I needed was a *kufeika*, a windbreaker padded with cotton. Then I wanted a winter cap with long earflaps, and finally some pants, also cotton padded. But the most important thing was the windbreaker to protect my chest. The wind was piercingly cold at night. Snow was expected any day now.

The reason we found out about our pay was that some foreman learned that our salaries were being handed over to the captain. What he, the lieutenant, and the interpreters did with the rest of the money after the rations for the camp were paid for, no one knew. It must have been a considerable sum, because each level had about ten prisoners, and there were six levels and three shifts a day. In any case, the foreman had reported his findings to Sirienko, and the two had complained to the *Golovoi*, and the *Golovoi* had called up the colonel in Almazna who was in charge of all the mine camps, and now we were to get our salaries.

In the middle of October we got an advance. I received one hundred rubles. A few days later, I went to the bazaar. Naturally, the prices in the bazaar were outrageous in comparison with the regular price of food when it was purchased with ration cards. For example: with a ration card, a kilogram of bread cost one ruble, whereas at the bazaar it cost thirty rubles. If a loaf of bread weighed three kilograms, then it would cost almost a hundred rubles, or about twenty-five dollars.

One *stakan* (about eight ounces) of tobacco was ten rubles, or about two dollars and a half. An old *Pravda* newspaper was between ten and twenty dollars. So smoking was expensive, too. The first time I saw the price of a quart of milk at the bazaar, it was about twenty dollars, but later it went down to ten. A *stakan* of salt was ten dollars. A *stakan* of sugar, forty dollars. Meat was so rare that one just didn't bother to ask the price. Clothing articles were also sky high. How those Russians managed to screw the prices up so much was amazing, yet there seemed to be no laws or restrictions to control them. It was a legitimate black market. After a while, I caught on that with a little bargaining, half the price could be paid in rubles and the other half paid by exchange for another article. The only problem was that a prisoner had nothing to offer as a barter. A secondhand windbreaker would cost me around two hundred dollars. Two hundred dollars, and I could survive the winter.

As much as I wanted my windbreaker, I ended up buying three *stakans* of cornmeal, a liter of milk, and half a *stakan* of oil. Then I rushed back to camp like a thief and cooked myself a brew, mixing the oil in with it. My body was starved for fat. I had fifty rubles left, and I figured that with my next pay I should have enough to buy a windbreaker.

According to the camp rules, each shift was allowed to go to the bazaar once a week, escorted by five guards. However, it soon became clear that this privilege depended entirely on the whim of the sergeant or on the guards themselves. Sometimes we didn't go at all. Sometimes when the guards were drunk or tired, they would walk the prisoners to the bazaar and then turn them around and walk them back, without letting them go in. So, as you can see, it wasn't a regular shopping excursion.

However, since I was able to walk back from the mine alone, I had developed the habit of stopping every few days at the bazaar. I admired and suffered at the same time by staring at all kinds of food and not being able to buy a thing. I always ran into some of my Russian friends there, but they weren't as friendly as they were at the mine or in their homes. I knew the reason; they didn't want to be seen with a prisoner. There wasn't a single family I had met who hadn't suffered a personal loss during the war. The fighting had just ended eight months ago. I understood that these people had reasons to resent me, some more than others, some less, but very few not at all, for I was a prisoner from an unfriendly country.

As I walked to the mine the day after the incident with Sirienko, I wondered how he would act toward me. I didn't see him during the first six hours of my shift, and after the first whistle sounded, I asked one of the girls whether she had seen him yet.

"No, I haven't, Vanya," she said, "but he's expected at the mine offices, and they also need him at the wood place."

Another carload of *poroda* came up from the mine, and I was on my way up to the tower to dump it out when I saw Sirienko coming down the road. He glanced up at the tower, and I looked away. I didn't want him to see me watching for him. He went straight to the mine office. After a while, another car came up, and on my way up to the tower I saw Sirienko coming toward the *atkatka*. He stopped at the blacksmith's shop, and when I was coming down from the tower I saw him. He looked a little sheepish and raised his hand in a wave. It made me feel good. He wasn't mad at me any more. When I got down, I went over to him and pointed to the tower.

"*Tovarishch* Sirienko, everything's in order up there."

"Yes, Vanya," he said, "I know you take care of your department when I'm not here. I wish I had more workers like you. Here." He handed me a ration slip for a thousand grams of bread. I thanked him, and he said, "Yesterday I was drunk. Forget what I said to you. I still have a headache."

I felt very happy. I went to unload some slag that had come up while I was talking to him. As I was going up to the tower, I saw him going down to the wood place, walking in his wobbling way. I loved him.

Chapter VIII

TOWARD THE END of the fall, Lisa, who also worked at the *atkatka*, invited me home for a meal. Of all the girls, she interested me the most. I sensed a deep melancholy in her and had a feeling that the endless hard work was slowly undermining her spirit. I wasn't sure why I felt this—perhaps it was because she seemed more intelligent than the others—but I often thought I could see her fading a little more each day.

She seemed pleased when I said I would like to come, provided I could get out of work details on my next day off. Lisa lived in the same village as Nikolai and Natasha, and she also knew the sergeant of the guards, who lived there, too. She said she would speak to him about it and make it easier for me.

The day before my day off, Lisa was at the *atkatka* and she said that she would meet me at the creek when the whistle blew the third time. I didn't tell anyone about it. I felt very tender toward her. The sergeant of the guards spoke to me the morning of my day off and told me that I should be back before dark.

When the whistle blew the first time, I went to the creek and sat down at my place. I started to think about Lisa. She had such wonderful soft blue eyes. In the West she would have been considered a rare beauty, but here in this dismal land she was only another girl who worked in the coal mine. I wondered about her home, and whether her mother and father would like me. Ah, what luxury I found myself indulging in! The formidable winter was knocking at the door, and here I was, dreaming sentimental dreams.

I went to the edge of the water, undressed, and washed myself thoroughly. Then I put my clothes on again and went back to my place under the trees.

As I turned around to sit down, I saw Lisa. She wore a plain white blouse and a dark skirt, and she had a red scarf around her neck. She really looked beautiful.

"How did you find me here?" I asked.

"I came a little early, and while I was walking along the creek I heard some splashing. When I came around the bend I saw you washing yourself, so I waited until you were through, and then I just followed you here," she answered.

As she told me this, I felt myself blushing a little. When she saw my face redden, she said: "I didn't watch you all the time. I just waited until the splashing was all over, and then I followed you at a distance."

I was glad that she had come early so that we could talk for a while. She sat down and I started to tell her about my home and how I wished that we could both be there together and that war had never happened in the first place.

Suddenly the third whistle sounded. It was three o'clock. She took my hand in both of hers while she just sat there and let me talk on and on. I never would have thought it could be so beautiful.

Then she told me a little about her family. Although everyone had worked hard before the war, it hadn't been as hard as it was now. Her father couldn't work any more because of his wounds, and her mother was sick, too. She had two brothers. The older one was an invalid from the war; he could hardly move his left arm and leg. The other brother was only ten years old. Except for her father's small pension and an equally small compensation that the older brother got from the government, Lisa earned all the money.

Before we left, I kissed her, and then she said that we had better go home, for her people were waiting and it was getting late.

The way she said "home" sent warmth running through my body. If only I could have found this girl in other circumstances, in another land...

She asked me whether it was really nice where I had grown up. She even asked me to teach her a few simple sentences in Romanian. She picked the words up easily, and in no time she was teasing me in her gentle way. *"Ce face baiat cu fata* [what's the boy doing with the girl]?," she would demand, and then laugh and laugh. I felt a tremendous surge of love for her.

Her home in the village was a small house like all the others. Her parents were very friendly. I could see that she was the pride of the family.

Her father had a strong, bearded face and clear blue eyes. He mentioned that Lisa had told him that Sirienko liked me. He said that that was good, because Sirienko was a very important man at the mine. Then we sat down and ate some good potato and cabbage soup. Lisa's mother filled my plate several times and said that I shouldn't worry about getting back to camp a little late, because Lisa had spoken to the sergeant of the guards about it.

My attention was on Lisa. In a way, these people behaved as if I was a suitor, but I was only a prisoner. They were wonderful people. Lisa must have told them kind things about me. After the soup we had kasha with fried onions and then some milk. Tea was served out of the samovar. The time passed quickly, and finally I had to leave. After I had thanked them, Lisa and I went out and she walked with me part of the way. When we parted, I kissed her once more. It was very cold, and I ran all the way back to camp.

And then the snow came. For three days and nights it fell in big flakes. Like everything else in huge Mother Russia, the winter came in a big way.

At home I had always looked forward to the first snow. Even now I liked to watch the individual flakes dance to the ground. If they fell on something warm, like the palm of a hand or a face—immediate death. If they fell on the white ground, on other flakes, they lived on until the warm spring killed them all. But this time the snow was a foreboding silence. While I worked up on the tower, I looked up into the sky, into millions of dancing flakes, and I thought they should all look black, as they would bring inevitable death to all the weak prisoners.

After it stopped snowing, the temperature dropped sharply. As far as the eye could see, a white blanket covered Russia. When the sun shone and I looked around from the tower on the day shift, the whiteness was blinding. If I looked at the bright snow for more than a minute, my eyes began to hurt. I wondered what it would be like on the night shift. I was soon to find out.

I didn't expect the tower to operate as well as it did, but there wasn't any trouble until a week later, when it got much colder and the snow became harder. During the next three weeks I really learned to hate that damned tower. Ten days after the snowfall I was rotated back to the night shift. The first night I had to unload sixty-four tons of *poroda*. The *poroda* car jumped the rails several times because of the ice that had accumulated on the track right under the chute where the *poroda* was dumped from the mine car. The only thing to do was to unload the car by hand, lift it back onto the rails, reload it by hand, and then take it up to the tower to be unloaded again. This took a lot of time; while I was working on the derailed car, sometimes ten or twenty other loads of *poroda* would come out of the mine.

The car jumped the rails three times that night. It was very windy. The snow sang and crackled when I stepped on it. My ears were half frozen, and my hands were numb. It must have been around 5 A.M. when suddenly I realized that Sirienko was watching me. He was standing next to the chute. I had no idea how long he had been there. When he saw that I had seen him, he scowled and said, "Vanya, at seven o'clock we'll go see if we can get something for you."

At ten after seven, when I had unloaded the sixty-fourth car of *poroda*, I was more dead than alive. I really felt it as soon as I stopped working. Sirienko took me to the mine's supply room. He issued me a fine Russian cap with flaps, which covered my forehead, head, ears, cheeks, and chin. He also gave me some gloves, made of strong canvas, and two new pairs of galoshes and some new canvas pants that were lined with uncombed cotton. What I really needed was a fur coat. All four of the Russians on the other two shifts had them, but Sirienko said he couldn't give me one because I was a prisoner. So that was that. I had spoken to Sirienko several times in the last months about my fear of the winter, and he had had too many things on his mind, but now it seemed that no matter what, I wouldn't be able to get a fur coat.

I made up my mind to get inside the mine, because spending the winter up on that tower would surely kill me.

There was a girl named Vasya who worked in the mine with whom I talked quite frequently. I found out that she had a cousin who was foreman of the sixteenth level. I decided to ask her if her cousin could do anything to get me transferred inside the mine. For there was one thing Sirienko couldn't do anything about: a foreman who was working on actual coal production was always given first choice of workers. Although I was doing a two-man job alone, it was still *poroda* and not coal. At that time the sixteenth level was the best producer in the mine, and this particular foreman was well liked by the *Golovoi*.

One night as I started my shift I had eighteen wagons waiting for me that the previous shift, with two men, couldn't unload. They were that far behind. So what could I do but start going up, rock the wagon once, shove hard and lift, and over it went; tilt it back and down. That shove and lift was becoming harder and heavier as I grew weaker, hungrier and colder. Every second day I asked Vasya, *"Nichevo novaya*—nothing new from Nikolaevich?" And so far her answer was always negative.

My new galoshes, which I had sewn together myself, were fine. They kept my *partyanki* (footrags) together. But naturally in the folds of the footrags, and the pants tied together with wire, there was always some snow. When I could step into the *budky* (shack), in the glare of the red-hot stove the snow in the folds melted. After two or three minutes I had to go out and make another trip, and the wetness would freeze in one trip. Those winds, those Siberian winds, they went through my backbone, through my empty stomach, howling and tearing and whistling, throwing snow viciously into my eyes and face. I used to think, is there a warm place left in this world, a place where you can eat as much as you want, so I wouldn't have to feel this horrible cold emptiness? Still, every day I told myself: after this winter I will escape. Just get through the winter. Just through this one winter.

And then one day, after his shift was through, Vasya's cousin came up to me.

"Vanya, did you work inside a mine before you were shipped to Mine 28?"

"Yes, Nikolaevich. I worked in Mine 31."

"As what?"

"As a loader."

"I know you're a good worker," he said, "but Sirienko will resist your transfer violently. Our only chance is that the *Golovoi* doesn't like him. Therefore he might transfer you. You will work well for me, won't you, Vanya, if you get transferred?"

"Yes, Nikolaevich, I'll do my best, as always. One thing: can you do me the favor of not telling anyone that I asked to be transferred, and just pretend that you want me because I'm a good worker? Otherwise Sirienko will be very angry with me."

"Of course." He winked at me and left, saying, "We'll know the outcome in a few days."

The next day there was a cave-in at the fourteenth level. A Russian and two prisoners got buried. They were dug out, and they were all dead, flat like three boards nailed together.

I asked myself what I was doing. Several of the other younger prisoners to whom I had confided my plans said that I was crazy to try to get into the mine. I understood them. It wasn't only the constant danger of working with thousands of tons of earth and rock over your head. I knew what a mine was like, especially a wet one. It was awful to come out into the terrible cold after having been rained on for eight hours. According to the prisoners, the climb out of the mine at the end of the shift was even more difficult than the hours of work. I agreed with them, but then no one knew what the tower was like without warm clothing. I really had no choice.

Two days after I had spoken to Nikolaevich, I sensed Sirienko's coldness. For the first time he passed without a *"Kak dela,* Vanya?" So I knew that the *Golovoi* had spoken to him and also that he suspected me of asking for the transfer, though he couldn't be sure. In any case, the battle was on. There was a lot of pride involved, because Sirienko usually got his way with the *Golovoi*. If it had been merely a question of one prisoner, even an important one, they probably wouldn't have wasted much time arguing, but there was a principle at stake.

The following day as I was coming down the tower I saw Sirienko approaching the *atkatka* from the direction of the *Golovoi's* office. He didn't greet me, but just swore something about when I was finished I was to go with him to see the *Golovoi*.

All day the nervousness built up in me, but at the end of my shift I suddenly realized that it was unnecessary, and for a minute or so a strange blankness came over me—I just couldn't have cared less what they decided. This passed as I was walking with Sirienko to the *Golovoi's* office, but I was still pretty calm. If they questioned me, I would answer them. I knew I was a valuable prisoner. The fact that they had called me to the *Golovoi's* office was something extraordinary.

When we arrived, I saw that Nikolaevich was also there. He was sitting in a chair. The *Golovoi* was seated behind a huge desk. He asked Sirienko to sit down, and he gave me a wink and a smile and said, *"Kak dela,* Vanya?" Then he turned back to Sirienko and said, "Why are you making all this fuss about one worker?"

"Tovarishch Golovoi, you know as well as I do what he does for me. I would need two men to replace him."

"But he is only a prisoner. How can he be so important, and why do you need two men to replace him?"

"I have two Russians on the tower this shift and two Russians there on the next shift. Sometimes they get stuck, but Vanya here never gets stuck. He manages alone. I tried to tip over the car on top of the hill myself, and I don't see how Vanya does it. He's just terribly strong, and I need him on the tower."

"But look how skinny he is. Maybe the four Russians are lazy. I don't understand it."

"Look, let's go right now, and you try yourself to tip over the car. I'd like to see you do it alone. Then we'll let Vanya do it, and you'll see what I mean. Let's go."

"You know I'm a busy man. If Vanya is such a good worker, let him work for Nikolaevich. Our sixteenth level is the best level. It gives us the most coal, and I think Vanya will do us more good there than if you keep him on the *poroda* tower. If you can't replace him, I'll give him back to you after a while."

"I don't know who is the cause of this, but if you take him, I want two other men, and I want them today. And I don't want them to be prisoners. I want them to be Russians."

"I'll see what I can do," said the *Golovoi* finally, and then he said to me, "See that you work equally well for Nikolaevich."

It was simpler than I had thought it would be. As we went out, no one said a word. Sirienko smiled a little, but he was quiet. Nikolaevich stopped outside and took me by the arm. When the door to the *Golovoi's* office closed, I felt that I had escaped a cold death. But I knew that my privileges were gone. No longer would I be able to walk back from work as I pleased. A pang of regret went through me.

Nikolaevich said that I was to start the next day with the first shift. He said not to worry about Sirienko, for he would probably get drunk today and then he would sleep like a lord and tomorrow he would be my friend again. Such optimism!

Book II

Chapter IX

I WAS READY for the mine again. I was sure I would hold my own, and that night I slept peacefully. At six in the morning I was ready to go to work with the rest of the prisoners.

The sixteenth level was the lowest. The levels started with the ninth, and went in pairs. The eleventh was the first level that was actually operating; the ninth level was caved in, and the tenth was used for storage. We went down by the ladders, which was very tiring and very dirty. I had gotten a lamp from Nikolaevich. It hung around my neck, and I breathed the fumes from the burning kerosene, an old familiar smell. When we got down to the sixteenth level, to my surprise I saw Lisa, working on the platform landing, handling the phone and the signals for the cars. She smiled and assured me that we would see each other just as often as before. Her friendliness eased my tension considerably.

The level I worked in was a dry one, and I fulfilled my norm of fourteen tons easily. I worked as a loader, shoveling the broken-down coal into a chute, with a big Romanian fellow named Omar. As we sweated and worked together, Omar became a close friend. I had to look around a bit to get a shovel as good as his. The one Nikolaevich had given me was too small. A shovel had to be huge, so that one didn't waste any strength. It had to be hidden, also, because workers were always looking for shovels, hammers, and long chisels. Even the best worker is practically useless with a bad tool. Omar showed me his hiding place, and I made it mine as well.

Three days after my transfer to the mine, I ran into Sirienko. He was talking to a girl, Katya, who was working on the landing. He called me over. He was slightly drunk. He showed me how after work I could jump between the cars on a train going out of the mine and ride to the surface. It would save climbing the ladders. Sirienko warned me to be sure to crouch very low, because once a Russian worker hadn't been low enough and a protruding brace from the ceiling had caught his head. The cars went about twenty-five miles an hour, and he had been pretty much torn to pieces by the time he reached the *atkatka*.

I was overjoyed that Sirienko was still my friend. I knew that the ride was strictly forbidden by him and by the *Golovoi*, ever since the accident with the Russian worker. After several months I could easily jump on and off a moving train both going up and coming down. Some of the Russians, including Nikolaevich, complained to Sirienko:

"Why do you let him do it? He might get hurt. And if you let him get away with it, why can't I do it? After all, he's still only a prisoner."

"Look, Nikolaevich," Sirienko replied, "Vanya can do it. I have confidence in him. He's very fast, and I know and trust him."

Losing Sirienko's friendship had been my biggest worry. Now it seemed that he still liked me. I doubt that he ever knew how much confidence he gave me.

I had entered a new world. After about a week on the sixteenth level, I felt accepted and even liked by all the Russian workers. Omar and I worked as loaders, or wherever else they put us. He didn't talk much, and there wasn't really very much to talk about. Yet in time we welded together into a well-coordinated team.

In spite of my fears to the contrary, I still retained my privilege of being able to walk back to camp alone. All the guards knew me, and it just didn't occur to them that I would contemplate escape. The fact that I now spoke Russian fairly well helped break down the barrier that faced most of the other prisoners.

Sirienko was standing at the *atkatka* one day when I came out after work. I saw right away that something was wrong at the tower. About twenty cars full of *poroda* were waiting to be unloaded. Sirienko said to me:

"Vanya, you see what has happened since you left me. I'm stuck with these Turks. I have two of them in your place, and since you left they've gotten stuck almost every day. Just look at all that *poroda*. Over twenty cars waiting to be unloaded."

"I'll go up with the next car and see what the trouble is."

On the way up to the tower I saw nothing wrong. The wind was cutting like a knife when I got to the top. As the car stopped, it started to slip sideways and fall off the rails. All this happened very slowly. I saw that one of the rails was a little loose. I dumped the *poroda* quickly. Just in time—for when the car was empty, its weight wasn't enough to press the rail outward. It ran down the rails smoothly. When I got down, I explained what was wrong to Sirienko. He sent one of the Russians to the blacksmith to get four spikes and a sledgehammer. As soon as the Russians came back I went up with an empty car and when I reached the spot I drove the spikes into the ties on each side of the rail so that it was secure. Then to make sure it was fixed I made several trips up and down the tower. Within fifteen or twenty minutes I had finished unloading all the *poroda*. The two Russians glared at me, while Sirienko cursed them.

Sirienko took me to the mess hall, where I was given a kilogram of bread and two hot plates of borscht. I was completely frozen. He mentioned again that I shouldn't have left him, but I replied, "Look at me, Vassilivanovich, I've been up on the tower for less than an hour, and I'm already frozen through. How would I last the entire winter?"

He nodded understandingly.

"I know, Vanya, but I can't do any more for you than I've done already."

In the bathhouse after our shift Omar and I would talk. For a while we discussed our work, but eventually…

"If we had meals here like we had at home," Omar said, "with a lot of fat and meat and potatoes, how much stronger we'd be, and how much better we could work!"

Our favorite discussions were about being home again and running into each other. We would cook and feast together. We invented dishes that no chef had ever even thought of.

Omar was a giant of a man, although he was extremely undernourished, like the rest of us. He seldom spoke in camp. He revealed a little of himself only in the mine when we were alone for a few minutes.

Together we shoveled coal for a month, and then we were transferred to work as *budshchiks*, shoring up the levels. During our month on coal, Omar and I made record salaries. We each received eight hundred and sixty rubles. The fact that we made so much money might have had something to do with our transfer. *Budshchiks* had a set salary. The quality of their work was judged by whether or not there were any cave-ins.

The coal vein was mined sideways. It was a layer of coal three to four feet thick, tilted at a forty-five-degree angle. That was why the mine was laid out the way it was, with the levels and the main slope at forty-five-degree angles. Every one hundred yards there was a level, because it was impractical for the individual levels to be any longer.

When a section of the vein had been excavated, something had to fill the void. The braces weren't strong enough to support the enormous weight of the earth, and as the ground began to settle, the beams would collapse. I once saw a brace the size of a man's thigh snap as easily as a man can break a matchstick with his fingers. So to support the ground, *budki* had to be built. They were solid walls of *poroda* six to ten yards wide and the thickness of the level which ran continuously from the main slope, where the mining had started. Every day, as the coal vein receded, the *budka* would be lengthened two or three yards on the other side of the level. No more than ten yards of level were ever left empty. The *poroda* necessary for building the *budki* was obtained by blasting out the spaces between them with dynamite.

Being a *budshchik* involved harder work and more danger than working on coal. A *budshchik* worked on territory where the ground already ached and groaned, and the braces creaked. He had to be twice as alert as a worker on the other side of the level. I constantly had sores on my back from jumping up suddenly. After every solid bump, I told myself that I would have to be more careful next time. But as soon as I heard a suspicious, cracking sound, I instinctively leaped up. I couldn't help it. Omar had the same sores in the same places.

The area above the *budka* where the *poroda* was blasted out was the only place where Omar and I could stretch out. It was a luxury to stand up and stretch once or twice before starting out of the mine. But we could never feel entirely at ease, because we had seen chunks of *poroda* two and three yards long drop down without any warning. They must have weighed fifteen or twenty tons. Naturally, if you were hit by anything that size, your worries would be over. Still, while Omar and I sweated together, nothing out of the ordinary took place, and the new job soon became monotonous and boring.

After the shift as I walked back to camp I would occupy myself with dreams. Unlike many of the prisoners, I had come from a home of books, and I had been a voracious reader of adventure and mystery tales. Now the stories stored up in my imagination—all the volumes of Sherlock Holmes, the Tarzan books, the exotic tales of Karl May—came to my rescue. I could and often did escape into those fantasy worlds from the dreadful drudgery and the sinking mental morass. The riches I had been given by those great writers kept my spirits alive.

That winter I began telling some of those tales to Getz and five or six others around the glowing camp stove. I told of Edmond Dantes, his cell in the terrifying Chateau D'If, his escape, and finally his revenge as the Count of Monte Cristo. They hung on every word, asking me, "Is it true? Is it really true?" And I always swore that it was. For that little time I took them away, and it gave me pleasure to transport them out of Stalin's paradise. Getz's eyes and his attention on me was the most rewarding thing I knew.

I had other, private dreams. I imagined that as soon as spring came I would approach Sirienko and tell him that I wanted to marry Lisa. after all Once back on the tower, I would start working two shifts every day. If I did the work of four men, it would only be a matter of time before I attracted the attention of someone important. Then my dreams promised that I would no longer be a *porodchik*. I would be in a position to help Lisa and her invalid father and sick mother. She wouldn't have to work at the mine, and she could keep house for me. I was sure that when I introduced Lisa to my mother, they would like each other, in spite of the language barrier. I don't know why, but I was sure that my mother would love her.

At times I clung to these dreams with a fervor close to desperation. Every day I had to face the hard, cold, brutal facts in the mine and in the camp, where the living conditions constantly grew worse and the morale sank lower and lower. There were more and more deaths.

One day before Omar and I left for the afternoon shift, the interpreter asked us to help him with some girl. For several weeks the girl had been in a stupor. Almost all of the women and girls were this way to a certain extent, but this particular one, the daughter of a professor from my high school, was much worse. She hadn't taken off her turban for months, and some of the other girls had seen lice falling from her neck. They told the interpreter about it, and he asked us to help him find out what was wrong with her.

We asked her to come outside with us. She refused. Omar had to carry her out, but she didn't resist much. The interpreter stood by while Omar held her, and I took her turban off.

Her head was a horrible sight. The lice were about half an inch thick. She was crying softly. The interpreter left and then came back with a pair of scissors, which he gave me to cut her hair. I stuck it into the mess of lice and just cut and cut. Then I gave the scissors to Omar, for I suddenly felt weak. I was holding her shoulders, and Omar kept cutting. The interpreter left and came back with some kerosene. He told Omar to wash her head with it, and even Omar the giant looked faint. I took the bottle of kerosene and poured it on her head and started to rub and scrub. The lice fell to my feet by the thousands. Her whole scalp was a horrible wound of blood, lice, and kerosene. Then a nurse came and led the poor girl away to one of the guards' rooms to take care of her. Half the population of the barracks was outside and had seen everything. The interpreter lit the crawling mass of lice and kerosene on the ground. I felt better as I saw those filthy animals go up in flames.

That was what happened when one stopped fighting back. But surprisingly enough, the girl suddenly seemed to recover, and after a while her hair started to grow again. The experience had probably scared her back into life. All of us had lice, and at the disinfection room next to the bathhouse the temperature was never right. It was either too high or too low. When it was too high it damaged the ragged clothes we wore, and when it was too low it was nice and warm and helped the lice multiply faster. The disinfection room became a breeding farm for lice. You couldn't do anything to fight them. If you killed one, ten took its place. They laid hundreds of eggs, and overnight you had hundreds of newborn lice. You couldn't kill them all, so you just shook out your clothes and the majority fell off. Every once in a while, you killed a few just to keep up appearances. I hated them.

Chapter X

SLOWLY THE COLD began to ease. It was very faint at first, but as the days went by there was less and less snow. The seemingly eternal enemy surrounding us was breaking camp and retreating. The first signs of green life were wonderful to see. Just as the year before, the spring seemed to lift everyone up. It gave us hope, and one began to hear occasional laughter around the stove again.

I had kept in contact with Lisa and the other Russian girls I had made friends with the summer before. They were working on the *plitas* (platforms) on each level, controlling the signals to the big *libyotka* that pulled the coal out of the mine. They were just as friendly as they had been when I was working for Sirienko on the tower—except for Katya, who was much friendlier. When she saw me she would let out a shriek: "Vanyushka, come here, let me see you!" She sometimes pinched my cheek, and when no Russians were around she kissed me twice. It left me shaken. I knew Katya was Sirienko's mistress, and Sirienko was my protector. Even though I had left him, I still depended on him.

I thought about Katya's frank approach the summer before. She had asked me straight out if I had been intimate with a Russian girl yet. When I said no, she had mentioned our taking a day off together. She would take me to her house, cook a good meal, and then we would make love. I had just blushed and laughed. She'd dropped the subject, but evidently she hadn't forgotten. Now she was hinting that we ought to get together on my next day off.

I couldn't see what she could possibly gain by making love to me. No one knew as well as I did how weak and undernourished I was, not to mention the dirt, the lice, and my ragged clothes. Even the poorest of the Russian girls, like Lisa, lived a much better life than we prisoners. If a girl had a lot of free time on her hands, I thought, the novelty of making love to a prisoner might attract her. But after walking several kilometers to work and working hard for eight hours, how could Katya have the curiosity or the desire? Or did she have some scheme in mind? I would have to be very careful, or the whole situation might explode in my face.

As starved and weak as I was, I hardly noticed that one woman was more attractive than the next. Yet I thought about the pretty German girl, Erika, who was still an *atkatchik,* working as hard as her weak condition allowed. Had she been as well-fed as the Russian girls, she would have had as attractive a figure as Lisa, but her body was skin and bones. Another of the German girls who had arrived with the group from East Prussia, a tiny, pretty girl, had become the mistress of the first interpreter. She didn't have to work, and within three months she had acquired a fat behind. But most of the women prisoners weren't menstruating any more because of malnutrition. I marveled at how Erika had survived the winter under the cruel working conditions of the *atkatka*. She displayed a lot of strength for a girl standing practically alone in this vicious fight.

Once when we had a little time to ourselves, Omar asked me off-hand what was between Katya and me. He had noticed once when she kissed me on the cheek. I told him about our conversation the previous summer. He said if I ever did anything with her, I had better be careful. I replied that I had no intention of doing anything with anybody. All I wanted was food, and if I could get a meal from her, why not take it?

"Including her," Omar said, and he grinned.

We had nothing to smile about, but his wolfish grin made me burst out laughing. We laughed so loud that Nikolaievich, our foreman, came into the light of our lamp and laughed too. "I couldn't believe that was you two," he said, shaking his head. "You're always so grim and quiet." After he left, we looked at each other and broke up again.

When the working day was over, I rode up between the coal cars. At the *atkatka* I found a beautiful, brilliant day. I looked up at the *poroda* tower and longed to be on it, now that the winter was over. But it would be useless to try to get back on the tower. Our foreman would never let me go. Omar and I had become too good a team.

There were now six Russians assigned to the tower, two on each shift. I asked the two Russians working there if I could go up and unload just one wagon of *poroda* for them. They said sure, if I wanted. I rode up and found that it was as easy to dump out the *poroda* as it had always been.

I looked around me. It was peaceful as far as I could see. What a fresh breeze! I looked up at the sun and thought about where I worked now, on the seventeenth level of that filthy, dark mine. I remembered how I had looked down at the workers emerging at shift change, crawling out of the earth like tired black worms. Now I was one of the worms. But I had gone through the brutal winter and I had survived.

I came down from the tower feeling sad. On the way to the bathhouse, Katya caught me and said she wanted to talk to me after I cleaned up. My soap ration had run out days ago, and the next issue was still a week away, but Vassily, the *kripelchik* (bracer), had a good-sized chunk and he let me use his. I put my filthy clothes back on and went outside. Katya was waiting. "If you had clean clothes on," she said, smiling, "you would be the most handsome man I know."

My cheeks felt hot. Then she asked when I had my next day off. In two days, I told her. But I reminded her that the guards were much stricter than they had been the previous summer. She flippantly replied, "I'll talk to the sergeant. You can spend your day off at my house and eat all you want."

That did it—*eat all you want.* This time she hadn't mentioned anything about making love, so I thought nothing of it—at least not consciously. But that sentence, *eat all you want,* had made me more aware of my gnawing hunger than ever. For the next two days I thought constantly of those words.

Katya was serious. The next day, I ran into the sergeant of the guards—not the friendly old man of the summer before, but a new one, gruff and serious. Yet he said, "Vanya, you can stay out on your day off. After you receive your bread ration, you will be excused from your details." (Now that I no longer worked for Sirienko, I had to do camp details like everyone else.) "You will go to Katya's. But you must be back before it gets dark, before eight o'clock."

I thanked him and thought, *eat all you want*...I felt like a traitor not telling Omar, but it would only have made us both feel worse. Omar was very reserved. He didn't make much contact with the Russian workers, though he handled the language very well.

The next day I walked to the mine with the morning shift. I ate my bread ration and drank my portion of thin soup, then went to the bathhouse and cleaned myself without soap as well as I could. I got into my filthy clothes again and sauntered over to the *atkatka* to wait for Katya, sitting on some braces that were waiting to be sent down into the mine. After an hour or so Katya showed up. Gay and laughing, she whispered to me to come with her.

Katya lived in a direction where I had not been before. She chatted gaily as we walked and told me she was living alone. She had her own little house, as she had been married very young and her husband had been killed in the war. She had no children, but she managed to have a pretty good time. Sirienko was a nice old man and treated her decently. She thought he must have a cold and cranky wife. She talked and talked. Then she asked me what I liked to eat. I said anything she ate, I would eat. Did I like to drink vodka? she wanted to know.

"No," I said, "I just like to eat a lot."

At that Katya grew serious. She said she felt bad that I was in the camp. Then, with a lot of zest, she cursed the war and its consequences.

We had walked at least five kilometers when a group of houses appeared on our left in a little valley. "We're here!" Katya said. "The second house on the left is mine." A few kids playing on the street greeted her.

We went into the house through a small foreroom, where there was a barrel filled with water and two benches with two washbasins standing on them. One of the basins was filled with dirty-black mine clothes soaking in soapy water. Then there was a large room one might call a living room, and a smaller room with a huge bed taking up almost all the space. Katya went into the bedroom, and I looked around. It was clean and neat. On a table in the living room were two *Pravda* newspapers, several bowls of flowers, salt and all kinds of cooking things, and two loaves of bread.

Katya came out of her bedroom. She had taken her jacket off, and under her plain white shirt I could see that she was a very healthy, well-proportioned girl. She gave me a pair of clean pants, saying, "They'll be too short, but they'll cover you well enough. Here is a shirt. But first go into the front room and put some water from the barrel into the empty basin. There is a big chunk of soap. Take your dirty clothes off and scrub yourself clean. Then put on the clean pants and shirt and come in. Maybe you can eat by then."

I felt a little embarrassed as I undressed, but to sit down on the clean blanket on the bench would have embarrassed me even more, because I would have made it black. The summer before, when I had been invited to Russian homes for meals, I had kept my clothes cleaner. It had been much easier, working on the tower.

I took a basin full of water, took my dirty clothes off, and with soap and cold water I scrubbed and scrubbed until my skin was red. Katya came in, and I blushed even redder. But she took the chunk of soap, and in a businesslike way started scrubbing my back. She handed me a large rough towel and went back to her cooking.

A little mirror hung on the side wall. I hadn't seen many mirrors in Russian homes. I took a look at my face. It was clean, but I had a lot of wild hair on my head, and I was very rangy and skinny. Whew! I was a sight! I couldn't understand why Katya liked me.

I put on the short pants and shirt and went inside. She smiled and gave me a comb, saying, "Go back and comb your hair, you'll look much better." I did, and it improved my drawn-looking face somewhat. We had a barber at the camp who cut everyone's hair every five or six months. I had last had mine cut about four months ago, so it was bushy, but with plenty of water I was able to part it. I had on white pants (even if they did come to just a little below my knees), a white shirt, I was fairly clean, my hair was combed, and in a few moments I was about to eat a huge meal. I didn't know of any other prisoner who could claim such good fortune, not even the interpreters.

Katya had cleared the table. A huge, steaming bowl stood on it, and two deep soup plates were filled with a delicious, thick bean soup. "Let's eat, Vanya," Katya said. "There's plenty of soup, and I have some other things for you after that I'm sure you'll like."

We both sat on the bench. The scent of the soup went into my nostrils. Oh, what a scent! Thick slices of pork were floating in the soup. I ate and ate. Katya filled my plate again, and a third time, while she had only one plate. Then she took the soup away and brought another dish over.

"It's rabbit stew," she said. "Eat all you want."

The rabbit was tender, the gravy was delicious, and there was plenty of it. My appetite seemed bottomless. Katya watched me eat, and it seemed to give her pleasure.

Finally I finished the stew and I was full, really, honestly full. My eyes still wanted to eat, to store up food, but physically it just wasn't possible. Katya smiled and said, "You did very well, Vanya. I enjoyed watching you eat as much as you enjoyed the meal. Let me wash the dishes, and then we can rest a little."

I lay down on the bench, but Katya protested. She insisted that I go inside and lie down on the huge bed. I had forgotten how soft a real bed is. What luxury, to sleep in such a bed every night. There was room for two more Vanyas.

I looked around. Facing me on the wall was an old painting of a half-undressed woman. There was a little dresser in a corner, and two chairs, and that was it—very neat and clean and decent.

Then Katya came in. She lay down next to me and said, "Now reward me with a kiss for the meal."

I blushed again and tried to kiss her cheek, but wherever I turned she faced me. So I kissed her on her lips. They opened into a ripe, passionate, wanting mouth. I was strongly aroused. Katya moaned and opened her blouse. There was no brassiere, only full, firm breasts, white and clean as snow. Her skirt somehow came undone while I was buried in her breasts, I lost my pants and shirt, and we became like animals.

After the first wave had passed, we looked at each other and smiled. I didn't know why, but I felt much better than I should have as a prisoner in the Soviet Union who had just made love to the mistress of his kindest superior. The outlook wasn't so stark any more; my balance was better.

We spoke of how it would be to live together, working on the same shift and walking to and from the mine together. She said, "Vanya, I would feel so much better taking those long walks with you in the winter. If you could get back on the tower and we could live together, you wouldn't be so skinny for long. You are so strong now—if I could feed you, you would be the strongest man at Mine 28! But if we were married, I wouldn't want any children, because then we would be chained to the mine. Sirienko sees to it that I never work too hard, but I hate the mine. You don't know how much I hate it. My father's father, my father, and one of his brothers died in that mine. Twenty-eight killed them all. I always wanted to leave the Donbas, but where can I go? I was married to a coal miner, he gave his life for Stalin and homeland—and I am *still* in the mine."

She snuggled up close and started caressing me with her fingers. Then she was all over me again, and I couldn't do anything but answer her passion. After it was all over I felt such utter exhaustion and healthy tiredness that I didn't seem able to move.

I must have fallen asleep in her arms, because when I woke up it was late afternoon. Katya was sleeping cuddled up next to me. Her face looked so peaceful, like a child's. But when I looked at her full, ripe body, I became aware of my own nakedness and quietly disengaged myself from her arms. I groped for my pants and shirt, which had fallen off the huge bed. As I was dressing, Katya'e eyes opened. She grinned at me. Then she cupped her breasts in her hands and winked. "Do you like them?"

"Naturally," I replied. "They are the most beautiful I have ever seen—but Katya, I am hungry again. And soon I have to go back."

She jumped up and pulled on her blouse and skirt. "I'll warm the rest of the bean soup for you."

She put some coal on the still-glowing stove and set the bowl of soup on it. Then she slipped on her shoes and said she would try to get some milk from one of her neighbors. I went back into her bedroom and lay down. What a soft huge wonderful bed! I was sure that very few Russians could boast of having such a bed.

Katya soon returned, singing and humming one of her sad, beautiful Russian folk melodies. I had heard her sing it before, but at the mine it didn't sound as beautiful as here, at her house. I was quiet, listening to her. I realized all of a sudden that I was really very fond of her. It made me sad, for it reminded me of my status.

She called me in. The soup was hot, and she had two liters of milk on the table and a fresh loaf of bread. Again I ate and ate and ate. Katya just watched me. She looked very happy. I must have appealed to her maternal instincts. When my plate was empty, she refilled it and told me to keep on eating. After the third plate all the soup was gone, but Katya brought me a chunk of salted smoked pork back, called *slanina,* and said, "You should like this." I loved it. After three plates of soup, a liter of milk, about a pound of pork back and a loaf of fresh bread, I was really full. I was embarrassed thanking her. "I want to do something for you, Katya. Tell me what I can do for you."

"You have done very well," she said. "Nobody has held me in his arms as strongly as you, and you are a prisoner. Now change clothes and leave, or I won't let you go! Here is half a loaf of bread for you, and another piece of pork back, and a chunk of soap. Take it with you, I know you'll need it more than I do."

It felt dirty to get back into my mine clothes and put on my filthy galoshes, but I had to step back into my place and face reality. The walk seemed far longer alone than it had with Katya. I looked at the moon, and it grinned at me in a friendly way, as if it knew what had happened. But then a dark cloud shut it off, like a warning. What if Sirienko found out? The next time they drank together and argued (and I had heard them argue), Katya might impulsively tell him about me. How would he feel about his Vanya then?

But what difference did it make right now? My stomach was full, really full. I had made love to Katya. I had a good piece of soap, and about a pound of pork back, which I would try to save for morning. I hadn't really done anything bad.

At the gate no one bothered me. The two guards nodded to me, and that was all. It was dark. Omar was asleep in the bunk above mine. When I saw his huge frame lying there, on an impulse I woke him. I asked him for the knife I knew he had hidden. He reached under his thin, straw-filled mattress and gave it to me.

I cut the pork back in two and offered him half. In the dark he took it, felt it, smelled it, then bit into it. Between mouthfuls he grumbled a touched "Thank you." I don't think it took him a minute to devour it all. Although I had filled myself twice, back in the starved atmosphere of camp I realized I was just as hungry as Omar. Not long after he had swallowed the last of his pork back, mine was gone too.

I told Omar where I had gotten the pork back. I had to tell someone, and I could trust no one else. He grinned sheepishly as I got to the intimate part of my story. "You have a lot of courage," he said. "I would have been afraid of Sirienko. Well, what's done is done. But be more careful in the future."

Several days later, I ran into Sirienko on the *atkatka*. He winked at me, grinned, and asked me how I was. Then he said, "Katya told me you were at her house."

I was dumbfounded. "Are you mad at me?" I asked him.

He laughed out loud. "Why should I be mad at you? You are young. If I should be mad at anyone, it's her, not you. It was she who invited you, and she gave you plenty to eat—so she told me. Then—she wanted you!" He shrugged. "She knows what she is doing. I knew before, when you were working for me, that she was curious about you and liked you. No, Vanya, I have nothing against her or you. Just be careful, so that the captain doesn't find out, because then I cannot protect you. So long, I'll see you around."

What understanding! I was lucky to have him. I felt much better about the adventure now. But the next time I saw Katya and she asked if we should take another day off together, I said, "Katya, please don't tell anyone. If the captain finds out, he might take drastic action. I'm a good worker, and I'm liked, but I am still a prisoner, and you are a Russian." She agreed, and that ended it.

l.

Chapter XI

THAT SPRING AND summer I really appreciated my freedom. I was able to walk to and from work alone, to go to the creek whenever I pleased, and to return to camp one or two hours after my shift had been checked in.

There was a guard who had been rather friendly, and one day when he was on duty I decided to ask him whether I could take Omar to the creek with me. I came out of the mine ahead of the rest of the shift and then walked from the *atkatka* to the hole in the ground where the ladders were. The guard was waiting for the emerging men. I asked him politely whether I could take Omar with me to the creek that day. I explained that we had both had a very hard time at work and that it would do Omar good.

"Let him go to the bathhouse," he answered me roughly.

What could I do? I must have looked very sad, because as I was turning around he said, "Vanya, remember that you will be responsible for him. If you really want to take him to the creek with you, I'll tell the guard at the gate in camp that you and Omar will be one or two hours late. Go. But remember that you will be blamed if anything happens, and don't be too late coming back to camp."

The guards looked up as we walked through the gate together on our return. I was glad to take Omar with me. From that day on, we went every second or third day. For five or six weeks everything was fine. As we loafed in the sun at the creek, Omar liked to speak of the past, although it inevitably saddened us both. But then Omar found another subject of conversation—escape.

I really liked Omar, but he was terribly introverted. I don't think anyone really knew him well. When you escape with someone, you have to know him well. Your life is in the balance. Physically Omar was reliable enough; but emotionally he was weak. In a tense situation he would require too much of my attention. I had to face reality: it would be too risky for two very big men.

After two or three weeks of hearing him talk about this plan and that, I grew more and more indifferent to his suggestions. Then in the middle of talking he would suddenly withdraw. Since I was far from enthusiastic about his schemes, I realized he might try to escape by himself. Then I would really be in trouble.

So, one day in the mine, I frankly told Omar that I couldn't take him to the creek any more, because he might be tempted to run off. I couldn't be responsible for him. If he tried to escape from the camp or from the mine, he had my blessings. If I could help him in any way, I would be glad to do so. As he listened to me, he nodded his head several times. Finally he replied, "In your place I would do exactly the same thing, so no hard feelings."

Then we shook hands. Omar made it easy for me by understanding my position. My respect for him increased.

Many prisoners had died. Over half the camp. Four hundred and fifty weak and sick weren't suffering any more. The spring halted the sickleman's harvest; for the time being, the warm weather beat him off. But his friend, the cold, cruel, all-encompassing winter, would join him again in a few months—just when we had had a little rest. A cruel alliance—winter and sickness. I knew I couldn't survive another winter like the last one if conditions didn't change for the better. The ranks of the prisoners had shrunk alarmingly, but no doubt another big shipment would soon arrive.

Sure enough, two weeks later there was a new transport. It came from the first camp. And with it came ten new guards, one of whom was the most vicious sadist I ever met. Usually a guard's shift lasted twenty-four hours, followed by a forty-eight-hour relief, but this new guard harassed dead-tired prisoners coming from work just for fun, even when he wasn't on duty. I saw him kick exhausted women, spit into suffering faces, and degrade in any way possible the most tired and weakest prisoners. But soon it began to tell on him. During the day he used up so much energy harassing the prisoners that he wore himself out. More than once, returning from the afternoon shift at 1 or 2 A.M., I found him sleeping in the guard shack when he should have been checking in the returning shift.

Twice this guard, whose name was Kolya, stopped me returning alone from the mine to ask me why I wasn't with the rest of my group. I replied that Sirienko had given me permission to go to and from the mine as I pleased. He had evidently heard from the other guards that I

had worked the tower alone, that I was a well-liked prisoner and one of
the best workers. He didn't like that, because he couldn't pick on me.

The second time he stopped me, the captain was at the gate by the
shack. I knew the captain liked me, even though he had argued with
Sirienko about my marrying a Russian girl. But that was in the past.
Now he smiled at me behind the guard's back, and stopped the inter-
view just when the guard asked me whether I thought I was a special
prisoner, to which I answered yes. The fact that the captain said nothing
about my going to and from work alone pleased me, but it further
angered the guard. The better mine workers were getting more and more
hostile toward this bastard. The other guards, the captain, the lieutenant, the administrators, and the interpreters must have noticed it.

Kolya was responsible for a frightening change in the late spring.
He argued with the captain and the sergeant of the guards until they
listened to him, and then he arranged permission to connect a wire
from one of the main electricity lines to the barbed wire encircling
the camp. He explained that it would prevent prisoners from trying
to escape or to sneak through and run off to the bazaar for half an
hour or so. I don't know how strong the electricity was, but it was
strong enough to make the posts around which the barbed wire was
wound smoke occasionally.

One day a dog was caught in the wires and was instantly killed. Two
days after that, one of the scrawny cows grazing outside the camp was
caught and killed also. People from the nearby village must have complained, because the electricity was discontinued. We thought that they
might give the dead cow to the prisoners, but we weren't so lucky. It just
lay tangled in the wire. Omar and I passed it going to work. On the way

back, it was gone. We were told that several villagers had dragged the animal away.

The road down to the mine ran alongside the barbed-wire camp fence. The mine was lower than the camp, so it was easier to walk to work than it was to come back to camp after work, tired, tired and dirty. After work the guards were not so strict, and the weary prisoners straggled out in a long line. At times some sat and rested. The hard part was to get up and start walking again. I was usually put at the end to keep stragglers in line. As the shift walked through the gate we were counted, going and coming.

One morning in the barracks we heard shots. We didn't know what it was, but as we lined up to be counted at the gate, we saw the mean guard Kolya outside the guard shack with his rifle ready. He had a board nailed to a post in the ground inside the camp fence, and he was having target practice.

The shift started walking. As we reached the end of the fence, I had an uneasy feeling...and then I got hit in the back. I was about to turn and see who had hit me when I heard the shot. I staggered a few more steps, and then—darkness.

The next thing I knew I was being carried on a couple of boards by two Russians and two prisoners, all the way down to the mine, to the first-aid room. The Russian nurse in charge knew me. "Vanya, what happened?"

"I don't know," I told her. She removed my shirt, and I saw a hole next to my left nipple. "I think I was shot."

"*Nu, pochemu?* But why?" As she bandaged my chest, I told her I had to go to work, my shift had started. "Vanya, you can't work! You've been shot right through your chest."

I still couldn't understand what had happened. There was a cot in a small room behind the nurse's office, and she told me I could lie down there. As I lay and rested, I realized that Kolya must have shot me. But why? What had I done?

The nurse brought me a cup of tea. "If you feel strong enough, you can go back to the camp. See how you feel tomorrow." I drank the tea, got up, thanked her, and walked slowly back to camp. At times I staggered, and I didn't know why. Then it came to me: I had been shot. I had a clumsy bloody bandage around my chest to prove it.

Kolya wasn't at the gate. Another guard there asked me, "*Nu*, Vanya, how do you feel?"

"A little dizzy, but all right," I told him.

"You don't have to work tomorrow," he said. "Go to sleep." So I did.

When I woke up towards evening, the left side of my chest was swollen and painful. All that night I tossed and turned. I must have had a fever. The next day when I took the blood-soaked bandage off, my left chest was even more swollen, and when I touched it, it hurt. In the afternoon I went down to the mine to see the nurse again. She cleaned my back where the bullet had entered, and then she cleaned the exit wound where the bullet had come out, next to my left nipple. She gave me two pills and told me to come back in two days. At the kitchen I got some soup, but then I realized that I wasn't even very hungry.

The next day I went to work with Omar. I just couldn't let him down. I couldn't do much, but I did what I could. My chest hurt more than it had the day before. What could I do? I kept going to work. Then I noticed that I had a very swollen left breast. After two more days, it opened up and foul-smelling pus came out. I went to the nurse, and she cleaned it up as best she could. After a few days she cleaned it again. I must have been healing, because my hunger returned with a vengeance.

Not long after, I was called into the captain's office. He had been away for most of a month, but as soon as he got back he had been told about the incident. He asked to see my chest. I took my shirt off and he saw the holes in the shirt, then the two wounds. He just shook his head. "If he bothers you again," he said, "tell me." And he gave me two big bread rations

One night around 2 A.M., coming back from the mine, I was following along slowly behind the shift when I heard someone whistle behind me. I stopped and turned around. It was the captain. He often took walks alone. I enjoyed running into him then, for when no one else was around, he spoke more freely with me. Once he asked me why Omar wasn't more open and talkative with the Russians at the mine. I told him that Omar just preferred working to talking, but I was surprised that the captain was so aware of Omar's behavior. After all, we were just prisoners. Good workers, yes, but still prisoners.

Soon we arrived at the gate of the camp. Kolya was sitting on the bench next to the shack, sleeping with his rifle between his legs. The captain whispered to me, "Vanya, are you afraid of him?"

"No," I answered, "but I am afraid of the small bullets from his rifle."

"Don't worry about that any more. Next time you find him asleep, tell me."

I said I would, and went inside the barracks to sleep. I could imagine what Kolya would do if I woke him up. And if I told the captain, Kolya would probably only lose his day off.

Time passed, and Omar and I were transferred first to the night shift, then to the morning shift, and then back again to the afternoon shift. My chest had healed, and I had forgotten all about the captain's order. I still walked back to camp behind my shift, and one nice, quiet night, there was the sadistic bastard, sleeping like a baby. As soon as I saw him, I remembered the captain's order. His quarters were about a hundred yards from the gate in the direction of the village. I decided not to ask for trouble, and I left the guard alone. Inside the barracks I lay down on my boards and went to sleep.

I couldn't have been asleep for more than half an hour when someone kicked me in the ribs. I jumped up and saw that it was the captain. He beckoned for me to come outside. I followed him, and once we were alone, he asked me harshly, "Vanya, didn't I tell you to wake me up if you found that parasite sleeping again?"

I said, "When I passed about an hour ago, he wasn't asleep."

He pondered and said, "Well, he's sleeping now. Come with me."

Silently we walked through the gate toward his quarters. The captain went inside and returned with a chunk of bread and a brand-new blanket. He handed me the blanket, saying, "Here. Take the blanket. Let's go back. You take the rifle from him quietly. Then give it to me and put the blanket over him and beat him up as hard as you can."

I was stunned. Fear and joy surged through me all at once. But fear was stronger, as I thought of what the guard had done to me and to some of the weak and sick prisoners. I didn't say a word, but just stood there. Then the captain gave me the chunk of bread, and without saying anything I started eating it ravenously. What could I do?

I crept up to Kolya stealthily. The captain stopped about ten yards behind me. I heard him chuckle. I looked at the sleeping guard's face. Even in sleep it looked evil. The rifle was between his legs and sticking out between his arms. First with two fingers I started to lift the gun slowly, and then with two fingers on the other hand. Little by little, I got the rifle away from him without disturbing his sleep. As the butt of the rifle came out of his arms, he grunted a little, but he kept right on sleeping. For a few seconds my heartbeat quickened. I turned around and gave the rifle to the captain, who was right behind me. He winked and told me to give the guard a good beating. Then I was to run to the barracks, taking the blanket, which I was to keep. It was as if a major in the army ordered you to beat up a sergeant. Naturally you had to obey the major because he has a much higher rank, but the sergeant lives in the barracks with you and is closer to you than the major. The major lives in officers' quarters, which often aren't even in the army camp or base.

I kept asking myself whether I would get away with the beating, or whether I would get caught between the switches. Still, I was very glad that the captain had selected me for the job, because I hated Kolya as much as he hated me. And to release some of my pent-up resentment against the whole camp could do me good. I looked at the miserable swine with pleasure. He was mine. He belonged to me. As undernourished as I was, and as weak as I felt, I knew that even if he had been awake, I could have destroyed him.

I put the blanket over him. The bastard didn't move at all. I put one arm under his knees and the other arm around his shoulders. As I picked him up, he started to move. I turned away from the bench with him in my arms and dropped him on the ground. Then I fell on his stomach with my knees in order to knock the wind and whatever courage he had out of him. When I heard his first weak cries for help, I started hitting as hard as I could in the direction of where they were coming from—his face.

I hit him blow after blow with every ounce of strength I had in me. I hit him for the bullet that could have killed me, for every prisoner I had seem him molest. I hit him for the hunger I had felt, for the miserable black coal mine, for the rotten interpreters, for the dirty, filthy, corrupt world we lived in. It was a nice feeling while it lasted. After a while I got very exhausted, and he started to grow lax beneath me. He had probably fainted. While all this was going on, I was encouraged by the laughter I heard coming from the captain, my only spectator. At the beginning his laughter had been subdued, but it had increased until it became almost a roar. If I hadn't gotten so exhausted, I probably would have killed the guard. But I didn't want to do that.

I didn't lift the blanket. I just got up and without even looking at the captain I ran as fast as I could into the barracks to my bunk and lay down. For no particular reason, I started to giggle hysterically. I couldn't understand why. I listened, and everything seemed quiet outside. After I had quieted down somewhat I went to sleep. I don't think I slept as deeply and soundly all the time I was in Russia as I slept that night.

The next morning Omar woke me up, which was surprising, because I usually woke him. My first thoughts were to try to picture what the sadist's face would look like. I hoped to find out on the way to the mine. I wanted to share my secret with Omar, for I was sure that he would appreciate my adventure more than anyone else. We had discussed Kolya before, and Omar hated him as intensely as I did. As we were walking through the gate, the sadist was standing at the door of the shack. He was a sight! His face was a yellowish-red and blue, and his eyes were growing into first-class shiners. By noon he would have a watermelon for a head.

I knew that as soon as we passed the gate, everybody would start to whisper question after question. I decided to tell Omar about it, and maybe some of the others, too. I thought it right for them to know that one of their fellow prisoners had done the damage. Let them see that we weren't completely powerless. When I told Omar the complete story, his one worry seemed to be that I hadn't beaten him well enough. He wished that he could have been in on the job. If he had, we would have killed the swine, for Omar was taller and stronger than I.

One prisoner told another, and by the time we were halfway to the mine, most of them looked upon me as a hero. The walk to the mine was like a victory march.

The eight hours passed very quickly, and I took the train out of the mine after work. I thought that I might run into Sirienko and tell him about the beating. I didn't see him that day, but I told him the story the next day. He asked, "Did you hit him hard?" and I said yes. He laughed, but not like the captain.

Back in camp I was a hero. But I had a feeling that I had done a foolish thing by letting everyone know about it. I hadn't seen the captain since I had left him the previous night, and I wished that I had, for it would have given me more confidence. I realized that previously days and even weeks had gone by without my seeing him, but I really missed him now. The sadist wasn't around, either. I had a faint hope that he might have been transferred.

Chapter XII

THREE DAYS LATER I was on my way to the camp after work, around 1 A.M. I had fallen about two hundred yards behind the shift. As I approached the gate, I saw Kolya standing in the door of the shack with his rifle pointing at me. He was grinning, and his face was still strongly discolored. He said, "Vanya, I have good news for you. Our captain has been transferred. He left several hours ago."

I knew then that he knew that I was the one who had beaten him up. There was no point in reasoning with him. Under normal circumstances he was full of lust and anger; now he was twisted by hatred beyond words The world around me caved in, but I don't think I showed it. That would have made him even more vicious. Behind him in the shack were two relief guards that I had seen only on rare occasions.

Kolya ordered me into the shack. The other two guards pointed their rifles at me and clicked the safeties off. The sadist pushed me into a corner, locked the door and said, "I could shoot you now and report that you tried to escape, but that would be too easy. I'm going to give you a beating every night when you get back from work, and eventually I'll kill you."

Then it began. I started to perspire. The sweat felt cold on my back. I tried to cover my face, but he hit me in the groin with his gun butt. I must have screamed, but I stopped, for he directed his kicks toward my face. Everything became hazy. Cold water was being thrown on me and then some more kicks and gun butts. When I tried to breathe deeply, I felt stabs of pain. Then there was nothing left but pain. The shack was empty, and I tried to get up, but for a while I couldn't. Finally, I dragged myself back to the barracks and fell on my cot, cursing myself into delirium. The pain became dull and throbbing and no matter how I moved, there were new stabs throughout my body. It would have been better if they had shot me, I thought.

I managed to get up and go to work the next day, and as I stumbled through the gate, Kolya was grinning at me from the door of the shack.

"I'll be waiting for you tonight," he growled.

That bastard, he was waiting for me already. He wasn't even going to take his forty-eight hours off. I didn't think I could take another beating. It would finish me, for sure.

In the mine I ran into our foreman Nikolaevich. I must have been a sight, for he shied back from me and asked me what happened. I told him the story and said not to be surprised if I didn't work too well. He said to do my best and if I couldn't do anything, that would be all right, too. He agreed with me that another beating like that would probably kill me or cripple me for good, and he assured me that he would talk to the foreman of the thirteenth level, who might let me spend the night in the small stable where they kept the horses. He was also going to talk to Sirienko and the *Golovoi* and see what he could do about getting Kolya transferred or punished.

I was bitter and cold inside, but this talk with Nikolaevich made me feel better. The reassurance that I would not have to go back to camp after work lifted me up somewhat. I tried to help Omar, but he wouldn't let me do anything. He managed alone. I was touched by his genuine concern for me. He wasn't a talker, but whatever he said, he meant. He was a giant in every way.

The worst pain came whenever I tried to take a deep breath. Omar insisted that in a few hours I should go to the stable and lie down. It would be better than staying in the mine, where I couldn't do anything anyway. He would see whether they would give him my ration of bread at the mess hall the next morning so that he could bring it to me.

I left Omar and slowly went along the level to the platform. The girl assigned to it was Katya. I had to tell her what had happened. I said that I was going to stay in the mine through the night and maybe for the next few nights, and she promised that she would bring me something to eat the next day. I was determined not to go back to the camp as long as the sadist was around.

I hobbled up the slope a hundred yards to the thirteenth level and crawled into the stable. It was empty. I lay down on some straw that was soggy with horse urine. What a pungent smell! I was very thirsty, and in a corner there was a pail of water for the horses. I drank some of it, but it was water from the mine and tasted dirty. I couldn't see much, for I had set my lamp as low as possible so it wouldn't burn much oil. I hoped that it would last me at least twenty-four hours. I tried to sleep, but I

kept thinking about the guard. Would they raise an alarm if I didn't
return to camp that night? Would they question our foreman?

In the midst of my worries I dozed off. I awoke when I felt a vicious
kick in my ribs. I screamed and saw that it was the foreman of the next
shift on the thirteenth level. As he bent over me with his light and saw
my bruised face, he said that he was sorry and asked me what I was
doing there. In the middle of my explanation Sirienko came into the stable and asked the foreman to leave the two of us alone. The foreman left,
and I saw that Sirienko had a small bundle with him He asked me to
crawl out of my corner so he could see how I was. He looked at me, and
then he gave me the bundle, saying that there was something to eat in
it. He said that Nikolaevich had told him the whole story. He also mentioned something about taking care of the parasite. That's exactly what
he called him, a parasite. But I knew there was very little he could do.
The camp wasn't under the mine's jurisdiction. He left, saying that he
would look in on me either before he went home or when he came back
to work the next day.

After he left I looked at the bundle, and as I opened it, hunger seized
me. There was about a kilogram of bread and a chunk of pork-back fat,
that precious fat. At the bazaar it was one of the most expensive items.

While I was gulping down the food, one of the horses was brought
back. They were being worked in twelve-hour shifts. Then I noticed several large rats. The horse was fed some corn, and the Russian who fed
them gave me an ear also. He left, and the rats stared at me as if they
were saying, "What are you doing here? You're a stranger. Give us the
corn. It belongs to us."

It was strictly forbidden to kill a rat inside the mine, for whenever a
cave-in was about to occur, the rats became very restless; they were used

as barometers of disaster. They were very big and ugly. There is something cold and very impersonal about the eyes of a rat that can send shivers down your spine. It doesn't happen when you're sitting in a nice comfortable dining room with a belly full of food, but when you're in a position where it is perfectly possible that the rats will start eating you, then it is time to give them some thought.

I dozed off and on during the entire shift, but was awakened again when they changed the horses. No one came into the stable. I would have ventured out onto the platform to see one of Sirienko's girls, but I was still terribly sore and bruised. The people of the coal mine were on my side. I was one of their best workers, and they would help me if they could. I drank some more of the dirty water and found a little dry straw. I made myself comfortable on that and dozed off again.

He came into the mine to look for me and found me in the stable. He had a strong, bright flashlight, and he directed its beam on me. I heard him shout with satisfaction and hatred. He put his rifle down, picked it up again, and came over to me. He kicked me once viciously and then started to hit me with the rifle butt right on my sore ribs. I screamed, and during the scream I had a weird hope that Omar would hear me and come to help. The sadist lashed and kicked. Then I saw Omar coming up behind him. He tiptoed until he was within reach of the sadist's back. In his hand he was carrying his mine lamp, which was made of cast iron. As he came close to the guard, he blew the light out, as it would have given him away. Then all of a sudden he was all over the sadist with his huge, terribly strong hands. Omar held him with one hand and bent him over his knee. With his other hand he gave him shattering blows in the small of his back. Then Omar straightened him up and gave him several vicious blows in the stomach. As the sadist yelled, Omar made a fist out of his hand which loomed like a terrible club over the other man's face. Then it dropped, and no more yelling was heard. But his cry had brought the guards into the stable. The sadist collapsed, and Omar tossed him aside. I had the rifle, which had been kicked in my direction during the tussle. It was half covered with my body, and as the guards came in I told Omar about it. He said to keep it hidden so they wouldn't see it.

When they were deciding what to do with us, Omar pointed the rifle at them and started laughing. Suddenly I laughed, too, despite my pain. Then Omar shot the first one and...

I woke up in pain and found myself still in the dark, stinking stable. Omar was holding my bread ration in his huge hand. It felt good to see him. He told me that the guards had wanted to give the alarm, but they hadn't because the mine was quiet. They were content with being told by Nikolaevich that I was around. They probably thought that I would show up sooner or later. Omar hadn't had any difficulty getting my bread ration. He told me to remain in hiding for a while, as he was sure it would be all right in camp. And it would worry the sadist not to know where I was, or who was hiding me. He knew that there were some pretty influential people around the mine who liked me, and I was sure this was bothering him.

The second day I became terribly restless, and I was sorer than the day right after the beating. Every move I made sent stabs of pain through me. I vomited blood and some sort of yellow saliva that smelled awful. Lisa brought me some bread. She was startled when she saw me. I had bloodshot eyes and sore, badly swollen cheekbones, and I hadn't washed in three days. But it was still me.

Omar brought my bread ration, and I complained to him about being sorer than on the previous day. He said to rest and not to go with him to the level to work. I grudgingly agreed, because I didn't think I would be able to manage it, anyhow.

I dozed off again and was awakened by Sirienko. He gave me some bread that I ate as quickly as I could. He said, "I have a surprise for you. I just saw the captain at his office."

I asked him to speak to Nikolaevich and ask if I could be excused right away. I had to go and speak to the captain immediately. Sirienko agreed with me. He said that Nikolaevich would excuse me and to go right away. I crawled out of the stable, stood up, and walked to the platform. A train of cars was coming up from the sixteenth level, and Sirienko ordered the girl to stop it. He motioned for me to jump on the train and then gave the two signals for it to start. I was on my way up, riding between the first and second cars. I turned my head toward the disappearing figure of Sirienko, and just before the dark slope swallowed me up, waved thank you.

When I came to the *atkatka* I was unable to jump off, but Nikolaevna stopped the train and I got off slowly. As I walked I was stared at by Russians and prisoners alike. I found that walking was painful, but not as difficult as it had been two days ago. I knocked at the door of the captain's office and heard his deep voice saying "Enter," which I did. He looked up, squinted his eyes, and said, "Vanya! What happened to your face? Did you get hurt in the mine, or did Kolya find out who gave him the beating?"

He put some fresh water in the samovar on the little potbellied stove he had in the corner behind his desk, and I started to tell him what had happened. When I finished my story, he picked up the phone and asked the operator for a number. Then he told whoever was on the other end of the line to send the guard Kolya down to his office. He would be waiting for him. Then he put the phone down and told me to take some tea and forget about the swine, as he would straighten things out as soon as he arrived.

I took a look at myself in the little mirror the captain had on the wall. I would never have believed a person could look so bad. My face was puffed up, my eyes were bloodshot, and my skin was all black from the two days I had spent in the mine. There was a piece of soap on the captain's desk, and I asked him if I could use it to go and wash. He said yes, but told me to finish within half an hour as he wanted me to be there when the guard showed up. I said that I would hurry, and went to the bathhouse.

It was about three hours after the morning shift had started, and the bathhouse was relatively free. I didn't have long to wait. I was filthy from head to toe. The soap and water did my bruises a lot of good, and I felt much better as I walked back to the captain's office. We had some more tea, and the captain assured me that after he had taken care of the guard he would send me over to the first-aid room to find out whether I had any broken ribs and get permission to take a few days' rest.

We heard footsteps. Someone knocked on the door, and the captain told him to come in. Kolya walked in, carrying his rifle. When he saw me, a hateful look came to his eyes. The captain asked him what was new in camp. Kolya said nothing, except for my absence. The captain told him to put down his rifle. After he had stood it up in a corner, the captain asked me to stand up. I did.

"Well, here is Vanya. Go ahead and punish him. Only remember that this time he will be able to defend himself."

Kolya looked at the captain and then at me and then back at the captain and remained silent. The captain repeated his order, but silence was the only answer. Then the captain screamed, "Well, punish him!" but the guard didn't move. The captain told me to sit down in the corner where I had been sitting before. He pulled on skin-tight gloves and walked up to Kolya and hit him flush on the chin.

Kolya staggered back and received another blow on his nose. Blood spurted out. Then the captain went wild. He hit the guard and kicked him until he was moaning on the floor. Then he threw some water on him and started cursing him as the vilest, rottenest, meanest parasite on earth. He cursed his mother, his family, Jesus Christ, and everyone else he could think of. Then he screamed at the guard to get up or else he would shoot him. When Kolya got up, the captain slapped him. The swine tumbled to the floor again.

"Never show your face again at this camp!" the captain said. "I'm going to transfer you, and if you ever show up here again, I'll shoot you on sight." Then he walked up to the prostrate guard and screamed, "I'll keep on kicking you until you get out of this office."

He started kicking, and the moaning Kolya crawled out pretty fast. I was perspiring and shaking. The captain told me to clean up the mess of blood and water on the floor. He had a mop in one of the corners, and I did the best I could. Then the captain took a bottle of vodka out of his desk. He poured some into a water glass and drank it and then offered me half a glass. I knew that it wouldn't be right if I refused, so I took it and drank it. It felt like drinking flame. My toes turned up inside my galoshes. I even forgot my aching body for a few minutes.

The captain gave me a note to take to the first-aid room and give to the nurse. I thanked him. In all honesty I told him that he had saved my life. He said that I would have nothing further to fear; as far as he was concerned, the swine had already been transferred.

I knew that I would never have to face that guard again. I had seen the fear in his eyes as he half crawled, half stumbled out of the office. In a way I was surprised, because I hadn't expected the captain to be so brutal. But then again, the captain's experience must have taught him that such people understand only the language of force, violence, and fear.

I went to the first-aid room, and the nurse was kind and friendly as she examined me. I sighed with relief when I found out that I had no broken ribs. She handed me a paper that gave me permission to take three days off. She said that I should wash my clothes and rest in the sun, if possible, and just let nature heal me. I couldn't wait to tell Omar what had happened.

Chapter XIII

THE SAME TRANSPORT that brought the sadistic guard had also carried a prisoner I knew from Brasov, my home town. He had come from Romania on the same train I was on, in a different car. His name was Puri. At home he had been a dancer with a bright future ahead of him. How terrible he looked! But we probably all looked the same way. When I asked him about conditions in the other camp during the winter, he gazed glumly at me and said, "Look at me and this transport. That's all that's left of us."

The whole shipment was in pathetic shape: ragged, undernourished, hollow-faced, sad. And these were the strongest prisoners. They were supposed to replace those who had died.

When I wasn't working, the few hours I had to myself I spent mostly with Puri. I would have liked to try an escape with him. I felt that I could rely on him more than on Omar. He wasn't as tall as I was, but he was very wiry and tough. In Mine 31 he had built himself a good reputation as a *budshchik,* and here in Mine 28 he worked on the thirteenth level.

Sometimes I met him on my way out of the mine, and several times I got him to ride up on the cars with me. But I always checked beforehand with the Russian girl on the platform to make sure none of the foremen were on the *atkatka*. I didn't try it often because it was too risky, but the few times I did do it, Puri was very grateful to me.

Then, whenever one of the more humane guards was in charge of checking the shift coming out of the mine, I would ask if Puri could come to the creek with me. I liked him a lot. He spoke Russian fluently, and in no time he became a favorite of the Russian workers, along with Omar and me. Actually, the Russians hadn't taken to Omar easily. They respected him, but I think they were awed by his size. His hands alone were grotesque in their hugeness. And when work wasn't progressing too well, he had a peculiar way of grunting before he said anything.

He seemed cooler toward me since I had told him that I couldn't take him to the creek, and when he saw that I was spending most of my time with Puri, he became more introverted than ever.

But even though we spent less time together at camp, we remained close. Working as a team in the mine had formed a special bond that could not be broken. Sometimes during our breaks he would tell me about his background. One day I learned that his grandfather had lived in a small town not far from Brasov where my own grandfather ran a restaurant, a *bodega*. Omar's grandfather had patronized my grandfather's *bodega* for years. Every morning about nine o'clock he had stopped in to drink a double *rachiu*. *Rachiu* is a strong, fiery drink made out of potatoes. After many years he had fallen ill, and a few days later had died. People insisted that the double *rachius* that he drank every morning had burned his insides out. But no one had ever seen him really drunk. This fortitude must have run in the family, for he was a physical giant like Omar. He was a very

kind old man, and he used to buy licorice for all the children in the
neighborhood. He had become a local legend when as a young man
he had once eaten about eight pounds of pork and beef roasted on an
open fire and had drunk ten bottles of wine, all in one sitting. Then
afterward, on a bet, he had danced for fifteen minutes with a two-
hundred-pound man sitting on his shoulders. He amazed everyone.
None of his excesses seemed to have any effect on him at all.

As he told me this, Omar said he could easily eat ten or twelve pounds
of meat, but instead of wine he would like to drink a pail of milk.

OMAR

I knew he could have done it; so could I. As he told me this, he
began to cry quietly with dry sobs, terrible sobs. He said we must stick
together and last through these awful times; we must conquer all the terrible enemies and get out alive. I had never seen anyone cry like that. It
was like milk when it reaches the boiling point, just gushing out. How
could he let himself go so freely—Omar, who was so introverted and
spoke so rarely?

Finally I said to him, "Look, we've come this far, we will make the
rest. We just have to last and make it. If two guys stick together, they
have a chance, even against the whole world."

He felt better then, and he admitted that talking so freely to me had
done him a lot of good. It made me realize that I didn't have anyone to
open up to, to talk to or even cry to. I hadn't realized this before Omar
poured his insides out to me. On the way back to camp, and that night
as I lay down to sleep, I thought about it, and I had to choke down sobs
for fear someone might hear me. I would have felt ashamed if they had.
I didn't trust anyone, not even Omar or Puri, enough to reveal my inner-
most feelings.

In the background I could hear the whining of the *libyotka* letting
empty wagons back into the mine. I hated that sad whining. Oh, how I
hated it. But when I think about it now, somehow it seems beautiful.

Throughout the summer all three of us continued to talk about
escape. In the sprawling Don valley there were many coal mines. The
best way to go was definitely by rail. To go on foot could only be done
at night and would be very complicated, for every large mine had a large
camp nearby with guards, and every day two-thirds of the guards had
their day off and they would all be snooping around the mine areas.
Even outside of the mine areas, there were many fields to cross. Each

collective farm had men patrolling every night. Although they weren't as numerous in the mining sections, they would still be a big problem. If we were lucky and did get out of the Donbas safely, we would then find ourselves on the banks of the huge Dnieper. If one was a good swimmer, it was possible to swim across it at night. I was a good swimmer, but Puri wasn't, and would never make it. Omar didn't swim at all.

To cross the river by the bridges was out of the question, because they were heavily guarded on both sides. Then there was the additional problem of getting a large supply of food together, which was close to impossible. No, the best bet was by train. A lot of the trains pulling out of the Donbas were headed west, where the Red Army was currently occupying many eastern European countries, which needed coal. But all the train stations were guarded, and whenever they had brought five or six empty boxcars to our mine to be loaded with coal, we had seen a guard come with the train.

As we discussed all the obstacles facing us, we realized that although things were much less guarded during the winter, winter was their strongest ally and our bitterest enemy. To underestimate the force of the winter would be fatal. So the best time was now. If we could have gotten the food together, we might have tried it, but we couldn't. However, that didn't prevent us from talking about it.

Toward fall our captain received a month's vacation, and another officer took his place. He was young, ambitious, and terribly aggressive. He was at his worst on Stakhanov days, and we had two that month. These were days when the work time and effort was increased to a frenzied pace to bring the amount of coal mined to the norm set up by the party. The days were named for a Russian miner, Stakhanov, whose daily output exceeded everyone else's by thirty or forty percent.

At these times the young officer would put on regular mine clothes and go down into the levels for several hours. Then he would return to his office, where he would drink his bottle of vodka and come right back down into the mine again. He would drive himself until the liquor wore off, and then he would promptly go out again, drink another bottle of vodka, and come back down again, just to make sure every prisoner filled his quota. Sometimes he would even grab the shovel out of somebody's hand. He would work furiously for an hour or so until he was exhausted. His special talent was cursing. He took God and God's family and stomped them into the mud. He was a raving, fanatical party member. He made it his duty to have one particular prisoner exceed his norm practically every day for four weeks. This prisoner was as strong as one could expect someone in our situation to be, and he was stronger than a lot of the others, but he was lazy by nature—or so the captain said.

Some days the new captain literally stood behind him in the thirteenth level for the entire shift. The poor guy wasn't allowed to stop working for a single minute during the entire eight hours, except to change to another spot where there was more coal to be shoveled. It was terribly cruel. At the end of the month he received a larger salary than he had ever received before, and the captain took all the prisoners outside the barracks, and told us that even the laziest prisoner can make a good salary, but he had to be driven to do it. Of course, he didn't mention that another month of the same treatment would have killed the fellow, without any doubt. After his spartan month his cheeks were so hollow and his face so pale that at night in the camp, or in the mine with his heavy lamp hanging around his neck, he looked like walking death.

Then three weeks later the prisoner came upon a can of fish that had been thrown into the garbage behind the captain's office. The captain and another Russian had eaten some of it in the morning and had thrown the can out. Seeing there was still one fish left, the fellow ate it. This happened at 3:30 in the afternoon, right after his shift was over. Back in camp he complained about having violent cramps in his stomach. Omar and I were on the night shift, so we left for work around ten. The prisoner had begun groaning dreadfully. When we got back from work the next morning, he was dead. Some of the prisoners said that before he died the noises and moans of agony coming from him were indescribable. He must have suffered terribly.

The fanatical young captain soon came up with another idea. He told the interpreter that after the next soap issue, which was in two days, he didn't want to see another dirty prisoner, meaning dirty hands and face. The joke was that the only clothes we had were the ones we had on. After working in the mine we went to the bathhouse and cleaned ourselves as best we could, but then it was just a matter of touching the rags we wore and our hands were practically black again. If you brushed off a fly or wiped an eye, your face was smeared right away. Nevertheless, whenever the captain saw someone he thought was dirty, he would assign him a detail. Naturally in a very short time he had the whole camp assigned to details except for the two interpreters, their mistresses, and one or two of the weak swine who had bribed their way out of working in the mine.

Omar and I tried to avoid bumping into the captain, but at least every second day we were caught and wound up cleaning some ridiculous part of the barracks with the rest of the prisoners. A special detail was created to dig behind the barracks for water. The captain said that he had a feeling that there was water there, and as long as he had the necessary men for odd jobs, why not look for water? So the project progressed until we had dug a hole eight feet deep, ten feet long, and ten feet wide. At that point the captain dropped the idea because not only was it extremely hard to get in and out of the hole, but it was practically impossible to shovel the loose dirt and gravel out. And so the project ended. But the fanatical captain didn't give up. He was constantly inventing new details. One day he passed by the bazaar and saw that the place was dirty. A few days later in the afternoon when the market was empty, he marched out a fifty-man detail, all dirty prisoners, of course, and gave them a little speech as a bonus.

"We citizens of the U.S.S.R. allow even you prisoners to take part in our bazaar. So, because we are so kind-hearted, I want you prisoners to clean up this whole area."

The crazy rat race went on for about two weeks. The captain didn't let anyone sleep. He would come into the barracks in the middle of the night and start shouting and cursing. Several times he marched the whole camp down to the creek at three or four in the morning to wash. Finally some of the foremen started asking questions among their workers, who were coming to work more tired every day. The foreman told the Golovoi about it, and the Golovoi called the captain to his office and told him to leave us alone.

On the last Stakhanov day, the young captain got what seemed to him a great idea. He decided to wake up the prisoners a little earlier so that they could work that much longer in the mine. In this way the glorious Soviet Union would receive a little more coal. I was in the shift that was finishing work when the next shift came in, an hour early, mumbling and cursing under their breath. They said that the captain had stormed into the barracks, and started gesticulating, ranting and raving at no one in particular. Then in the middle of his tantrum a piercing scream had torn loose from his throat, followed by some wild curses. "You lazy swine, sleeping instead of working for the great Soviet Union and Stalin who gave you world peace." It was such nonsense, but he believed everything he said.

A few days later our captain returned from his leave, and the fanatic was transferred. I felt sorry for the young officer, for there was no way of knowing what he had gone through in the war that had made him so crazy. But I felt even sorrier for the prisoners in the next camp to which he was assigned.

It took a few days for the tension to wear off. Then a certain peace settled over the camp. Vassily, the young Russian timberman, invited me to his house for dinner. He lived in the barracks behind the mine. I had been there the summer before. His brother wasn't at home, for he was working in a different shift, but his mother was there, and she made me feel wanted and comfortable. We ate only borscht and kasha, for they were a struggling family. But they were very decent and honest. They were both concerned, and even angry, that none of the prisoners were allowed to get mail from home, but they were hopeful that things would soon become better, for it was already fifteen months since the war had ended. Still the drive for coal and the misery remained the same. Undoubtedly, conditions would improve, but the Russian people had gone through a terrible war, terrible suffering, like the rest of Europe. The aftereffects were as bad as the war itself. It would take years to heal the scars, especially in the Donbas, but if conditions at our camp and at the mine remained the same, none of the prisoners would survive another winter.

Still Vassily and his mother gave me some hope. I just had to pull through. At times I thought about confiding in Vassily and asking for his advice and help concerning an escape. But I knew what he would say before I asked: Don't try it. He liked Sirienko very much, and he knew that Sirienko liked me. If I tried to escape, then some blame or suspicion would be put on Sirienko, because he boasted so much about me. The military might think he had helped me in some way. Even Vassily and his mother would be under some suspicion.

After dinner I thanked them, and then I walked to the creek. I wanted to be alone for a while. There was a chill in the air; soon it would be winter. During the cold months the hunger gnawed more than ever at my insides. It was vicious, that cold, empty hunger!

One detail that had been assigned during the reign of the fanatical young captain was repairing a cellar about ten minutes away from our camp, near the bakery. It was a huge cellar, and it had been used during the war for distributing vegetables, potatoes, and cabbage. A detail, including some Russian carpenters, had repaired it so that it could be used again this coming fall and winter. Just as the fall began, the local farmers started shipping in the products from their harvest to be stored for later distribution. I noticed truckload after truckload of potatoes being stored away. It gave me an idea. The next time I returned home from the mine late at night I stopped and looked at the lock. It didn't seem too complicated or difficult. I knew that Puri knew something about locks, and a few days later I found him at the camp after we returned from work and told him about my plan.

If the lock was carefully opened and closed, we would be able to help ourselves several times.

Puri went to look with me. After a glance he said, "Let's do it tomorrow. All you have to do is talk to the guard and arrange it so I can walk
back from work with you. If we manage to get in, we can hide the potatoes in our clothes and boil them in the camp."

The next day I asked the guard to let Puri stay with me.

"Borisovich in the kitchen has some work that has to be done by
morning. I want Puri to come along with me, for I need his help."

I knew that the guard would consent, and he did. Half an hour after
the shift had gone back to camp, we left for the cellar. We slipped down
to the entrance, and Puri started opening the lock while I stayed on the
lookout.

In a few minutes he opened the door and went inside. Lights were
unnecessary, since we were used to the darkness in the mine. He
stashed as many potatoes inside his clothing as he could and then
came out and took my place at the lookout while I went inside and
filled my clothes. Then I came out again and watched while he closed
the lock. We casually strolled back to the camp. The guards nodded
as we walked in. We went straight into the barracks and baked our
potatoes on the fire. No one watched us. Naturally we were so fam-
ished that we just couldn't wait until they were done, and as a result
we started eating them half raw.

We were interrupted by an interpreter who sauntered into the
barracks. He stopped at the fire, saw us devouring potatoes, and asked
where we had gotten them. I said that we had done some work for
Borisovich and he had given us some potatoes in return. It didn't
sound too good, because anyone that helped fat Borisovich got fed

down at the mess hall, but at the moment it was the only plausible thing I could think of. The interpreter left the stove where we were sitting, strolled around a bit, and then went back to his quarters. Puri looked at me. I shrugged my shoulders. We finished the last of our potatoes and went to sleep.

I slept soundly, and when I awoke the next morning I noticed a commotion in the interpreter's quarters. Puri and I paid no attention to it and went to work as usual. However, when we returned to the barracks after our shift, the interpreters called us in and questioned us about the potatoes. Of course I kept insisting that we had worked for Borisovich and that he had given us the potatoes. We were interrogated separately until morning, and then they brought us in together. They said that someone had stolen some money from their quarters and that was why we had potatoes. Since payday was only a few days away, no one ought to have any money; the only way we could have gotten any was to steal it, and that explained how we had gotten the potatoes. They searched us several times, but they couldn't find money on either one of us. This confused them completely. But then they said that we must have hidden the money somewhere down at the mine and that we would have to be very careful until payday, for if we splurged a lot of money, it wouldn't go unnoticed.

What could we do with those two bastards? They threatened to involve the captain, and they said they would even question Borisovich to find out whether we had really worked for him or not. That was all we needed. Finally we told them where we had stolen the potatoes. It worked. They let us go, saying that they would think of a suitable punishment.

We continued our daily routine. Finally, on payday they caught the thief. He was an old man who was very sick. He had tried to bribe a guard with a ten-ruble note a day before payday to let him go to the bazaar. Since he was old and sick and very weak, he had probably given the interpreter a watch or something to get out of working in the mine, where he would have died, anyway. The guard whom he had tried to bribe became suspicious, and after accepting the money and giving the old man permission to go to the bazaar, he went and told the interpreter. The poor old man returned from the bazaar about two hours later. He had gorged himself with food, and he brought back some cornmeal, pork back, sugar, and two *stakans* of Mahorka tobacco. He started to cry and admitted to everything.

They took their seven hundred rubles back, as well as the Mahorka, sugar, cornmeal, and pork back. If they could have taken the food he had eaten at the bazaar from inside his stomach, I'm sure they would have done so. As a punishment they put the old man to work at the wood place behind the mine where the braces were cut. Three weeks later he died.

For stealing the potatoes Puri and I were forced to dig two hours a day in the hole where the captain had made us all look for water.

Three days after Puri and I had completed our punishment, I met Vassily on my way out of the mine. He asked me to come over to his house to have something to eat. Omar had already left, and I climbed out of the mine with Vassily instead of going up with the cars. We were alone in the bathhouse, and I told him the story of our potato robbery. I knew he would understand, and he did. Then he told me about an article he had read in *Pravda* a year ago, about a mine about fifty miles east of ours, which had owed the party a great deal of coal. The authorities had summoned all the available workers from the neighboring farms to come and work in the mine to help them pay off their debt. This happened right at harvest time, and as a result the potatoes were never harvested. Vassily couldn't remember the estimate of how many thousands of pounds had been left in the ground. It seems unbelievable to me that they would let those potatoes rot, when rations were so low. Vassily had told me the story so that I wouldn't feel bad about the potatoes we had stolen, but it only made me angry.

Later, at his house, Vassily showed me a photograph of his mother's father. It was an old, yellow, stained picture that showed a wrinkled old face with a thick beard and very bushy eyebrows. Vassily told me that his grandfather had loved to take walks in the snow; sometimes he had walked as much as fifteen miles at a time. When he returned from these walks, his beard would be heavy with ice. Vassily would help him pull off his boots and then pick off the beads of ice.

Whenever I went to his house to eat and talk with him a little while, I would feel good, but at the same time a little sad. A lot of the prisoners felt only hatred when they spoke about anything connected with Russia. But they were wrong. The Russians were people just like everyone else. There were good and bad among them.

If the physical hardships hadn't been so severe, there would have been herds of psychopaths running loose in the camp. I don't think there was one prisoner an honest medical board would have declared sane. Half the prisoners didn't care any more what happened to them—they were too beaten and sick and weak—and the other half knew that the coming winter would prove fatal.

As I walked to and from work I noticed that the two Russians working on the tower were already wearing their fur coats. The top of the tower was now about ten stories from the ground. The night winds from the northeast were already very cold, but every once in a while a wind broke in from the southwest, from the Black Sea, and this gentle breeze felt like a message of warmth from home. Still, this limitless land would soon be covered with a white blanket of snow.

Chapter XIV

THE RETURNING SHIFTS from the mine were stopped at the gate, and every prisoner who didn't bring back a good-sized chunk of coal was punished by being assigned to some detail or other. A supply was being stored up so that when it suddenly got cold all the camp fires and stoves could be kept burning around the clock. Some nights the temperature was already below freezing. In the morning the fields looked white with frost, but within two hours they would turn to a yellowish-green color. The sunflowers in the fields smelled of decay. The stems were dying, and the first heavy snowfall would finish them off. The evenings were endless. The Russian girls at the *atkatka*, whenever they had a chance, sang beautiful, sad folk songs. In the background was the sad whining of our winch, joined by the fainter and even sadder whining from the winch at Mine 68.

When one passed by the platform, one could sometimes hear the Russian girl in charge singing along with another girl, who was in charge of the next platform, a hundred yards up or down the *uklon*. The areas were lighted by electric lights, and they could see one another only faintly and yell back and forth. They usually communicated by phone, but whenever they weren't busy and no drilling or hammering was going on, a group of them would get together and sing.

There was another Russian girl named Dusya who usually worked on the thirteenth or fourteenth level. She and Lisa, Marusya and Nina were great friends, and they loved to sing together. Sometimes they arranged to work the same shift, and then, since they lived in the same village, they would harmonize as they walked to and from the mine. Dusya was tall and slim, a fiery, dark-haired, attractive girl. She and Lisa were the best-looking girls in Russia, I thought, if only they could have been groomed and properly looked after. With the hard labor and coal dust and the shapeless mine clothes we all wore—men and women alike—it was very hard to keep any feminine touch. Dusya always wore a bright-colored kerchief tied tightly around her forehead that accentuated her high cheekbones.

At times when there was a lag in production, a lack of empty wagons to be filled, or ten or fifteen minutes off because of blasting, the younger Russian workers in the mine would play around with the Russian girls. Verbally, they were very rude. Some Russian girls coped with this better than others, but no one did it better than Dusya. Whoever used language that reached "below the belt," she had a way of looking at him that just froze him. Fiercely she refused to tolerate such things. I loved that in her. Once when I was present, a *desyatnik*, or sub-foreman in charge of ten workers, said to her frankly, "I'd like to f—k you." Dusya looked at him and remarked, "I don't think so," and turned her back to him and started talking to me, totally ignoring her superior. That showed a lot of style, con-

sidering my status as a prisoner and the status of a *desyatnik* of a top-pro-
ducing coal vein. She was a thoroughbred.

The harvest had been good, and all the Russian workers had some
potatoes, corn, and sunflower seeds stored up. They began to take their
heavier clothing out: fur coats, caps, felt boots, and windbreakers, which
every one of them had. To see a Russian outside in the winter without a
windbreaker would be like seeing a coal miner without a lamp. With the
prisoners it was a different story. The food was usually much better in the
summer and fall than in the winter, which didn't make our chances of sur-
vival any better. The clothes issued to us were the same all year round.

Some additional workers were brought to our mine, but they
were Russians, not prisoners. They had been soldiers during the war
and had been taken prisoner by the Germans. After the war was over,
several of them told me, they were thoroughly screened. If the
Russian officials thought that they had seen too much of the Western
way of life, they weren't allowed to return home, but instead they
were assigned to some work gang. Our additional laborers were all
such people. Now they were forced to join us at Mine 28. There was
a lot of bitterness among them, which was understandable. A few
were still full of life, glad that the war was over. Others didn't care one
way or the other. Most of them turned out to be good workers. One
of them, whose name was Mischa, was put to work on the thirteenth
level, and our foreman introduced him to Omar and me.

Mischa was one of those warm, talkative young fellows who make
friends quickly with everyone. Quick to smile, quick to show sympathy
and understanding, he was a very intelligent, alert young man. The first
day Nikolaevich introduced us, we became friends immediately and

went to the bathhouse together. We didn't have much time to talk, but every day before or after work we tried to see each other.

Then one day I was standing with Mischa in the bathhouse. Omar had already left. Next to Mischa were the clothes of another one of the former war prisoners. Mischa looked around and saw that this other fellow was in the shower. "Come here," he whispered to me.

While I watched, he quickly went through the other man's clothes and put something in his pocket. It was a little steamy because of the shower water, and I couldn't see what it was. Mischa told me to get dressed quickly and come over to the mess hall, where he would get me something to eat. He was acting very strangely. He left, and I slipped into my clothes and galoshes and caught up with him near the mess hall.

"You didn't see a thing," he said. "You were standing beside me all the time."

"Fine," I shrugged. "I didn't really see anything, anyway."

Mischa gave me his ration of bread and a plate of borscht, and then he left. He said that he was going to the barracks. I knew that he was going to hide or sell whatever he had taken.

I was still eating when several Russians came in from the bathhouse. They asked me whether I had seen Mischa or knew where he was. I told them that he had gone home. Then they asked me what I had seen him do while I was near him in the bathhouse. I said that I had seen nothing unusual. Suddenly one of the Russians pointed at me and said, "It's you who took the watch!" So that was what he had stolen!

"Search me if you want to," I told them.

Just then Borisovich came out of his kitchen and asked what had happened. They told him.

"Don't abuse this particular prisoner," he said, pointing at me, "or the *Golovoi* will get angry." So they apologized to me and told me to tell them if I happened to hear that anyone was trying to sell a watch in camp. Later I told Omar about the incident. He told me it would be safer for me if I didn't talk to Mischa too often, for he was too smooth.

During the next two weeks we heard that several other things had been stolen from the barracks where the ex-soldiers lived. I knew who the thief was, but he was too clever to get caught. He probably sold the goods at the bazaar, or had them taken to the bazaar in Rovenki, eight miles away. Once the goods were converted into rubles, he was safe.

I saw Mischa two days after the incident with the watch. He grinned and said, "I heard what happened after I left the mess hall. Don't worry. I'll see to it that every time I'm able to I'll get you something extra to eat."

Then he showed me his ration card, which had half a loaf of bread left on it, and said that he would give me the bread. At the mess hall he paid for the bread and handed it to me. Then we spoke for a little while, but we didn't have much time, for he had to be on his way and I had to go back to camp.

"Too bad we're in such circumstances," he said.

Several days later I saw him at the mess hall. He was drunk. He seemed a little belligerent and unnecessarily loud. I decided to say no more than "Greetings, Mischa," and "How are you?" whenever I met him. He was too dangerous, despite his pleasant personality.

Although the ex-soldiers were Russians and were better fed and better treated than the prisoners, they still suffered from the strain and hardship of working eight hours a day in Mine 28. It showed in their faces and bodies. Only the local people, the natives of the Donbas, seemed to be able to stand the driving pace and the brutal working conditions. Suffering told its tale on them, too, but they were conditioned to such hardship, for their fathers and grandfathers had lived in the same way. The only means of livelihood these people had was the coal mines. A man at the age of thirty-five looked fifty or fifty-five. I had the impression that the coal was branding them. After years of working in levels for eight hours every day without being able to stand up and stretch, it seemed that their back muscles were like bands of steel.

The Russians complained, but their complaints were mild because they feared the state and the party. We prisoners had no right to complain about our rations, for Stalin had made a law that gave us the same rations as the Russian miners. The only difference was that the Russians *received* their rations. Except for the bread, which we got regularly and in the right quantities, our rations were cut or stolen, and often disappeared before we saw them. But whom could we complain to? The Red Army? Administration? I didn't even know where the administration was, for camps such as ours.

As the weeks dragged by, it became colder and colder. The snow hadn't fallen yet, but the cabbage soup became thinner. Here and there, prisoners began to die. They had to be buried, of course, and once again it became one of the cruelest details. A place had been picked out last winter in the frozen ground behind the camp, and this winter it was the same place and the same tiring task. It was almost impossible to dig even a very shallow hole in the frozen ground. Each grave was marked with a stick so that no one would accidentally dig there.

Omar and I were in the afternoon shift, from 3 p.m. to 11 p.m. It hadn't been too cold when we went into the mine, and the eight hours passed quickly. We finished our *budka* and as we were leaving the level the night shift coming in told us that a snowstorm was raging outside.

Omar and I took a train of cars out of the mine, which we tried to do as often as possible in order to save our strength. Outside, we stepped from under the roof of the slope right into a blizzard coming from the east. The snow was already over a foot deep in some places, and in other places where the wind had blown the snow away, the ground was hard under our feet as we walked. Although the bathhouse was only three minutes from the *atkatka*, we were cold and shivering by the time we got there. We cleaned ourselves and went out into the storm again to the mess hall to try and get something to eat. The thought of the mile-long walk back to camp wasn't too pleasant. Winter had come in a grand style. It hadn't come quietly; it had come in with anger, angry because it hadn't been able to come sooner.

One day Omar and I finished our work about an hour earlier than usual. We weren't able to get anything more to eat at the mess hall than our customary plate of cabbage soup, and afterward we were hungrier than ever.

Our captain had been back from leave about two months. He had brought a nice round, fat dog from home. During the last two months Borisovich had fed him because he was the captain's dog. He was even fatter now than when he first arrived at the camp.

Usually we didn't see the dog at night when we returned to camp, but that night as we walked through the gate, there he was, playing in the snow. The door of the guard shack was closed, and we could see the guard through the window, asleep in front of the glowing stove. Omar looked at me meaningfully. I wasn't sure what he was thinking, but I had an idea of my own. However, we were once again thinking the same thing, because Omar bent down, and the dog came to him playfully. Then...crash...Omar hit him with his mine lamp. The force of the blow made Omar lose his balance and fall. I picked the dog up and put my windbreaker over him. I walked to the barracks, with Omar behind me.

Everyone was asleep. I was amazed at how quickly Omar skinned and separated the dog with his knife. Strip, rip, cut…and soon it was over. The stove was glowing brightly, filled with white-hot coals, and the dog's intestines, fur and head burned quickly.

I brought in some snow, which we melted in our pots. After five minutes we had divided up the meat and put it into the boiling water. Omar had some salt hidden away. We divided that, and our dinner soon began to smell delicious. After half an hour or so, Omar started to eat his portion, and I joined him. To us it tasted like regular meat. We sucked the bones while the glowing coals reduced the remains of the captain's dog to ashes.

A few days after this, one of the Russians asked us to help put up a supply tent next to the mess hall. They had already started driving in the posts, but the ground was very rocky and frozen under the snow. The fourth post would not go in at all. The Russian who was swinging the sledgehammer was growing more tired with each blow. Then another Russian, one of the blacksmiths, grabbed the sledgehammer and started swinging as hard as he could. At the second blow the handle of the sledgehammer cracked.

There was a small rail tie lying nearby. Omar picked it up and walked over to where the fourth post was to be placed. He looked toward me, but I was already walking in his direction. I held the post while Omar swung the heavy tie with anger. With each blow the post went into the ground about half an inch, and after about fifteen blows it was in far enough so that I now longer had to hold it for him. I let the post go and stepped back to watch. The Russians had gathered to see the spectacle, too. And it was a real show. Back home, people paid money to see such a performance. The Russians wouldn't even have thought of using the tie; normally it was carried by two men. Yet this giant was using it as a sledgehammer by himself.

Ivan Ivanovich was shaking his head and smiling to himself. I knew for sure that by tomorrow every Russian in the mine would know about it. Ivan Ivanovich called to Omar to stop. Omar obeyed and angrily tossed the tie to one side. Then he stepped back, a little embarrassed as he became aware of all the stares directed at him.

We pulled the tent up, which took only ten minutes. Ivan Ivanovich said that our job was done. He told the Russians that if they wanted to eat something, they should come along to the mess hall.

In the kitchen Ivan Ivanovich spoke to Borisovich. He must have told the fat chef what Omar had done, because Borisovich came out with two plates of kasha for Omar alone. The plates were really full. We ate and ate, but as hungry as I was, I couldn't help watching Omar and thinking about how he had swung that tie, his powerful arms and shoulders, his huge chest. How starved and undernourished he was, and still he had such strength! If they fed him regularly, I thought, he would be the strongest man in the world.

Right after the brutal entrance of winter, one of the prisoners received a letter from home. It was heavily censored and not very readable. We asked him how many times he had written home. He told us that he had given a short letter to a Russian co-worker, who had mailed it for him, and then he received the answer. The only thing one could learn from the letter was that the fellow's wife and parents were still alive and that his child had been born several months after he was arrested. It was a boy, and he was healthy. Several prisoners had tried corresponding with their people back home, including myself, but to my knowledge he was the only one who ever received an answer. He tried to write back, but his Russian friend said that he could no longer help him; he had been told that it was forbidden. So the matter ended with that.

Poor-quality writing paper, which one had to purchase in order to try to write home, was occasionally seen at the bazaar, but it was a very high-priced item. A pencil was also an expensive item, and the quality was very bad. It seemed hard to believe that a pencil cost ten rubles. At home one would have thought nothing of a pencil, but after all, conditions were different here. When I thought about my life now, the life I had led at home seemed like a fabulous fairy tale.

During the last two or three weeks Omar had warned me at work that I wasn't as alert as I had been. You had to react to every noise the ground made. When the ground ached and moaned, you had to listen and try to understand. It seemed to me that the ground protested against our taking the vein of coal out of its bowels. And especially against our taking it out so rapidly, never really giving the ground a chance to settle on the squarish *budki* we were building. On our level, which was producing the most coal, the *budshchiks* were under constant pressure to keep up. In fact, it was impossible for two men to build a sufficient length of *budka* in eight hours to keep up with the coal production. It would take about ten hours every day. Fortunately, Omar had been shown by some of the Russian *budshchiks* how to cheat a little. This is what we did.

First we laid the wall for the bottom of the *budka*, and for two or three yards of the side wall, up the level. Then we filled in the space, just as we would normally, and after that we laid the rest of the side wall, another three or four yards up the level. With some loose rocks and old braces we would build a wall parallel to the bottom wall, and perpendicular to the side wall about a yard from the top. This created a center space in the *budka*, three yards by three yards, which was empty. As soon as this extra wall was built, we would shove *poroda* in as fast as we could to fill the remaining space. From the outside it looked solid, and when the *budka* was completed, it was impossible to check to see whether it was done correctly.

Naturally, what we did was dangerous, for when the ground eventually settled on these half-empty *budki*, it would squash them, and it might cause a cave-in. But filling the *budka* completely with *poroda* was impossible. Omar and I sometimes had to cover ten yards in one day, and it was humanly impossible to do even eight yards in eight hours. All the *budshchiks* cheated, although not as much.

Omar warned me again about not being alert. He knew more about the interior of the mine than I did, for he had worked inside the levels since we had arrived at Mine 28. I had a lot of faith and confidence in Omar, which was one of the reasons that I wasn't as alert as before. The second reason was that I wasn't eating in Russian homes any more and was considerably weaker.

One afternoon we had just laid two meters of the side wall, when Omar snapped at me, "Come on, stop dreaming and get out of there."

I shook my head and cursed myself. Then I heard Omar scream, "Jump out!" I was in front of the empty *budka*, sitting on my haunches and leaning against a brace. I heard him yell again, "Jump out! Jump out!" and then I felt a blow on the back of my head—and then nothing…nothing…

Chapter XV

THE NEXT THING I was conscious of was climbing a ladder. Up and up and up. I thought that I should have reached the outside long ago. The mine had never seemed so deep. Then I realized that I had a sore head and I couldn't move. I could breathe, but my legs were clamped down as if they were caught in a vise. Suddenly I realized that I had been knocked out and that I was just coming to. I was buried in a cave-in.

How was it that I was still alive, could still breathe? How long would I be able to breathe and to live? Had the cave-in occurred throughout the entire level, or was it a minor one, like the cave-in a week ago at the sixth *budka* on the thirteenth level, in which no one was hurt? This mattered terribly. If it was minor, I had hopes that they would look for me.

I tried to move. Impossible. I tried to wiggle my toes, but they seemed to be numb. Then plain, naked fear overwhelmed me. I cried and then screamed, but I only succeeded in filling my mouth with coal dust that threatened to choke me. It looked as if my time was up.

My childhood really did parade past me. I remembered finding some wild strawberries miles away from home in the forest. I had plucked them and brought them to my mother inside a large green leaf. As I gave them to her (I knew how she loved them), she looked at them, the very first strawberries that season, and then gazed at me a long time. Her eyes became moist, and I turned away, embarrassed. I didn't want her to cry. I only wanted to make her happy. I remembered that look she had in her eyes. It seemed to be the most beautiful and tender thing I had known in my life.

But then I came back to the present. No matter what I thought about, I always came back to the present.

I couldn't understand how I could breathe. It wasn't fresh air, but at least it was air. I lost all track of time. I felt the sweat running down my face, and it was tickling me. I had a strong desire to scratch my nose, but I couldn't move my hand. I cried again, wondering at the same time why I didn't feel hungry. As soon as I thought of it, I did, more than ever. If I could just have one meal, a good meal before I died.

Up until now I had felt physically comfortable, except for the strong headache that had awakened me. But now I felt a dragging pain increasing in my right calf. Breathing was becoming more and more difficult. I was gasping…I couldn't take any deep breaths. I was in a cramped position and there was a lot of pressure on me, and I wondered how much longer I would last with only these short gasps of stale air. I thought I would suffocate. To me there was no death more dreadful than suffocation. I forgot the pain in my legs…and then I kept trying to straighten my position, and as a result I felt new stabs of pain and had to take more gasps of air. Dust filled my mouth each time I gasped. The perspiration continued to flow; my exhaustion increased...but I still remained in the exact same position.

How long had I been here under the rocks? Was it a day or two, or only eight hours? I couldn't tell. Fear choked up in me again. Then I thought of praying to God. Maybe that would help. But...no! It wouldn't do any good; it never had. The weaklings had all prayed from the very beginning and they had withered wearily away and died.

Suddenly I heard a faint, faint noise, a noise only a scraping shovel could make. Then it grew quiet again. I stopped breathing and concentrated with every bit of strength I had left in me and listened...but the only thing I could hear was a grumbling moan of the ground every now and then, and between the moans...deathly quiet. But what could it have been? Was it only my overwrought senses? I concentrated again, and...yes, there it was again. Now I was sure that someone was shoveling slowly toward me. I would have liked to bet that it was Omar.

I scarcely breathed in order to listen. Then I heard a second shovel at work, too. Little by little, the noises were growing louder and louder. It seemed that the pressure around my legs was getting lighter. Then I felt an object being pushed toward the toes of my right leg and I tried to move my leg with all the will power I had left in me. The object was pulled away, and the shoveling increased. The scraping noises doubled, and then I realized how hard it was for me to breathe. If those noises had stopped, I would have died. Then, suddenly, I was able to move my toes. I heard Omar curse and say in Russian:

"Come on. Faster. He's still alive."

Then I felt a hand on my right foot—pulling it gently. It hurt, but I didn't care. Three shovels were working now. My knees were freed, then my thighs, and finally I could stretch my legs. Omar grabbed both my legs and gently pulled me out.

I couldn't believe it. By the light of several mine lamps I saw Omar panting and several Russian workers, including Vassily and Sirienko, standing around me. Sirienko, I found out later, had supervised the whole thing. Omar, I was told, had worked like ten men. I looked at him. He grinned, and he had tears in his eyes. I had tears in mine also, and I just couldn't say a word. It had been long, terribly long. I had thought days had passed, but it had only been four hours. I just lay there panting. There are no words to say how good it felt to be able to breathe freely.

I asked Omar whether my hair had turned white, as I knew fear could do such a thing. But he just poked me in the ribs and grinned, saying, "No, you're just the same as you always were."

It was unbelievable. Some minutes ago I had thought that my time was up. Considering everything, it didn't look as if I was hurt very badly. I had an ugly cut on my chest from a jagged piece of *poroda*, but the bleeding had already stopped. Yet, no matter how I moved my legs, I felt an intense pain. I didn't think any of the bones were broken, but the pain was dull and constant. I also had a few minor scratches on my face and arms. I had lost my galoshes, but Omar had found them in the loose *poroda*. My jacket and pants were torn. I was lying down about ten yards from where I had been buried. My rescuers were standing around me. They, too, were afraid of the mine. It showed on their faces.

"One can never be careful enough," Sirienko said, "especially when one takes the coal out as fast as we do. The mine is dangerous, Vanya. I've spoken to you many times about it. One can't rely on it. You have to be alert at all times. Omar told me that you haven't been as careful as you should be. You were lucky this time, but never fall asleep again, especially while you are working as a *budshchik*."

Then he asked me whether I could crawl slowly down the tunnel to the level, where they would put me in an empty car and push it to the platform. Omar offered to help, but I said that I would do it alone. I crawled slowly and stopped several times to thank the Russians who had helped dig me out. They followed me until we reached the level.

As I crawled out of the tunnel I had to jump down to get to the level, for the entrance of the tunnel was five feet from the floor. I didn't want to cry out, but I really felt like it as I jumped. Stars glimmered in front of my eyes. Something was wrong, very wrong with my legs and feet!

"Vanya, sit down in an empty car," Sirienko said. "Omar will push you to the platform."

"No," I said, "I want to do it alone. I can make it if I go slowly."

"Don't be so stubborn," Omar said. "Take help when it's offeredto you."

"I have to make it myself, Omar," I answered, "so that I can feel what is really wrong with me. There's no other way to find out than to go and walk myself. In case I can't make it, you'll help me."

It was painful, every step of it, but finally I arrived at the platform. I sat down in an empty car that had been hooked onto a full train going out of the mine. Outside I saw only a dreary light, and large flakes of snow were falling, but to me it seemed better than a sun-filled spring morning. The Russian workers, among them Lisa, Nina, and several other girls, fussed over me and let me know that they were glad that I was all right.

Omar helped me get out of the car, and with me leaning on him for support, we started out for the first-aid room. It wasn't far. With Omar's help it was easier for me to walk than it had been in the mine. Also, in the daylight I could see where I was stepping. But it was still painful, and I had to walk very slowly.

As we passed by the mess hall, a guard who was waiting for the shift to emerge from the mine told Omar to go back to camp, that they would take care of me in the first-aid room. So in front of the first-aid room Omar started to leave, but before he did, he said to me:

"I know you would have done the same for me. Take care of yourself and if they send you to the hospital in Rovenki, see that you send word to me how you are doing."

Then we shook hands and looked at each other, and we could both feel the questions that were in our minds. Would we see each other again? Would they send me to Rovenki, and after that, what? Would Omar survive by himself?

As Omar stalked off, I felt alone, more alone than I had ever felt before. I had no one to lean on but myself, and both my legs were terribly wounded. I staggered into the first-aid room. The nurse was friendly. She knew me, for I had been sent to her when I was shot and beaten by Kolya. Sirienko had been in before, and he had told her about the cave-in. She told me to lie down so that she could look at my legs. She touched my right calf and then increased the pressure slowly with her fingers. I begged her not to press, for the pain was brutal.

I couldn't understand it. I was pretty sure that no bones were broken, since I was able to walk. But there was so much pain! Finally I begged her not to touch my legs any more, or I would just scream and die. She wiped my forehead with a towel. The pain had made me cold and clammy with sweat. She gave me three pills to take. Then she left, and shortly she returned with hot soup and some bread.

Everything seemed drowsy and blurred. I remember that the soup tasted much better than the soup the prisoners were normally fed. I ate it and thanked her, but I spoke slowly and in interrupted sentences, only half conscious of what I was saying.

I had been sitting on the couch, and she told me to lie down again. I did, and began to think about what would happen to me now. She hadn't told me anything about my legs yet. As I wondered, I dozed off.

A fine train came to a stop at the coal-loading platform of our mine. My father got off, dressed in a glittering uniform. Several Romanian soldiers got off after him, and they came to get me. They carried me to the train on a stretcher. The Golovoi *came out of his office with Sirienko. The captain of the camp was with him, along with several of the guards. They demanded that my father's detail tell them where they were taking me and what authority they had to do so.*

The soldiers put down the stretcher and my father started to explain to them in Romanian that he had every right to take me home because I was his son. I would get well at home, and then I would return and work for them again. The look in Sirienko's eyes told me that he would let me go, but then he looked at the captain. I knew all along that it would be up to the captain, and not Sirienko, to make the final decision.

"Vanya," the captain finally said to me, "this man is on Soviet territory and he can't take anyone away from here."

I told this to my father, and he remained silent for a few moments. Then he said: "We will fight. We won't give up so easily. After all, we out-number you, and I think we can win. The train will take us away quickly, but we'll have to start shooting right away."

The Golovoi *interrupted this by saying:*

"Captain, perhaps you should let him go. If Vanya here promises that as soon as his legs heal he will return to Mine 28, I think it will be all right."

The captain looked pensively at the Golovoi *and at Sirienko. Then he nodded his head and said:*

"Comrade Golovoi, if you will take the responsibility for it, then it is all right with me."

As I was thanking him I saw a train coming at full speed toward the train my father had arrived on. They collided with a terrible crash...Smoke...commotion...my father's soldiers...Russian soldiers...the Golovoi...Sirienko...the captain and my father were all a blur before me. I saw blood, heard screaming, felt the earth move as in an earthquake. Snow...ice...coal...poroda...dead prisoners...pain...

I was in a white-painted hallway on a stretcher. There was a pungent smell of medicine. I realized that I was in a hospital. I saw three nurses at the entrance door and recognized one of them as a nurse from our camp. The other two were old Russians. They walked over to my stretcher and Regina, the nurse from our camp, saw that I had my eyes open. She smiled at me. After the dread I had been through, it felt so good to see an attractive face smile. Yet it seemed so out of place that I asked her why she was smiling.

"Because the nightmare is over for you," she answered. "We came here by train, and it must have been very painful for you with all that shaking and bumping. You moaned and groaned constantly and you even talked to your father in your sleep. Then you spoke to Sirienko, and you screamed. But now you're in the hospital, and I think you'll be taken care of here. I have to return to camp, but every once in a while we'll get word to you. If I can get permission, I'll stop by myself occasionally. Take care of yourself."

Then she spoke a few words to the Russian nurses and left. I tried to get up, and finally after a ten-minute struggle, I managed it by leaning against a wall. The nurses had all disappeared. I fought the faintness and finally got up and walked toward a door. A nurse was just coming out, and she was surprised to see me standing up. She gave me her hand and led me inside a ward.

There was a stove by the door. All the beds except two were occupied. She took me to the nearest empty one, which was the fourth from the door, and I slumped down on it. It had hard springs and only a thin mattress, but it felt like a sultan's couch. Every part of me seemed to ache. I just lay there and rested. I still had my clothes on. Drowsily I remembered that someone had told me to undress. After I had taken my clothes off, I shoved them under the bed and kept right on drowsing.

It was between day and night—first half darkness, then complete darkness, surrounded me. I couldn't see anything except a dim light burning in the corridor. The silence was interrupted only by an occasional groan from one of the other beds. I felt a strong need to urinate. I got up slowly and felt my way toward the dim light in the corridor. Suddenly, realizing I was naked, I turned back and groped for my pants and galoshes under the bed. I put them on and continued on my way out. I went along the hallway to the entrance door and then went outdoors. I urinated against the wall. When I returned to the ward, I saw some clothes hanging on the wall next to the door. As it turned out later, they belonged to other patients.

Nobody seemed to be in charge. If I had seen a ghost, I wouldn't have been surprised. I noticed all these things, yet I was so drowsy that even the pain I felt seemed miles away. I lay down. The drowsiness became thicker, until I couldn't remain conscious any more.

It must have been about noon the next day when I awoke. The first thing I felt was a constant, dull, drumming pain. It came from my right ankle and calf, and in weaker throbs from my left leg, also.

Our ward had two windows that were all frosty. Everyone huddled under blankets, but to me the temperature seemed comfortable. There were about fifteen beds in the ward, and all but one were occupied. My neighbors on either side seemed to be asleep, but the one across from me asked me how I was. He called me by my Russian name, Vanya. I must have looked surprised, for he began to explain that a brother of his had worked with Sirienko in the mine many years ago. They still saw each other from time to time, and that was how he had heard about me. When the nurse came in earlier, she'd said that the *Golovoi* had called up from Mine 28 to see that I was being taken care of. He told me that they had never had a prisoner from Mine 28 in this hospital before.

I told him that I was fine, although my brain was still a little foggy. Suddenly he yelled, "Marushka!" which was the nurse's name, and she came in to see what was the matter. He told her to bring me a bread ration. She saw that I was awake and came over to see how I was. I said that I was fine, and she left. She came back a little while later with an older woman who was carrying a bowl of hot soup and two hundred grams of bread; that was the ration for the patients. The nurse went to look at some of the other patients while I ate.

Then she returned and said to me, "Tomorrow our doctor will be here, and he'll examine your legs. But right now I want to dress the cut on your chest."

The rest of the afternoon was spent quietly. In the long, long evenings the patients talked to each other. The only interruption was supper—a thin barley soup and sweetened tea. Three bulbs lit up the ward. At nine they were turned off. I didn't think of being bored, for it felt so good just to lie there, not having to think of the next shift, when I would have to get up and go to work. My whole body was as heavy as lead from fatigue and overwork.

Then I wondered what the doctor would say in the morning. The throbbing in my legs was still there. It felt like a growing infection. But it was only the beginning of an infection, so it wasn't unbearable yet. For the time being I could rest comfortably, and to hell with tomorrow.

Everyone in our ward had to go outside to relieve himself. There was an outhouse about thirty yards from the entrance of the hospital. As my legs swelled up and the pain became worse, I started to count time by the trips I made outside. It took all my strength to control myself and hold back my screams. I had to walk with the slowest, smallest steps, steps which demanded the least movement possible. When I got back to my bed after half an hour of the most horrible, painful walking, I would slump down, my clothes soaked in cold sweat, utterly exhausted, dreading and fearing the next walk outside to the toilet. I would hold myself back as long as I could.

The first few days I spoke to some of the Russian patients, but after that, I was conscious of nothing but the terror of the pain—pain that crept closer and closer as it came time to urinate.

About six days after I arrived at the hospital, Regina, the camp nurse, visited me with Omar. I never knew how they managed to get permission to come, but all of a sudden, there they were looking at me. They came just at the time when I was concentrating all my strength and energy on getting up and starting my journey. I nodded to them and said that I had to go outside to urinate and that it was very painful to move my legs. They both said they would help me.

"No, no," I said, "the nurses have tried to help me already. They had me lean on them, and I walked slowly, but it wasn't any help, because I still had to move my legs."

Omar said that he would carry me. I said no, but he just picked me up and walked slowly outside. The Russian nurses came in at that point and remarked how wonderful it would be to have Omar there as a male nurse, because he was so strong.

Outside the hospital Omar stood me up, and after I had urinated, he carried me in again. Regina was talking to the younger Russian nurse. They both came over to see my right leg. I tried to roll up my pants, but they were too tight. The Russian nurse told me to take them off and she would bring me a clean pair and a clean shirt as well. She left, and I told Omar to rip them at the seam, for I was embarrassed to undress in front of Regina. Omar did so, and the calf on my right leg was bigger than my thigh and really red.

The Russian nurse returned with a pair of standard pants and a shirt. She said that I could change into them after my visitors had gone. Then she explained that the inside toilet was frozen. The upstairs one was in working order, but they had no room for me upstairs. Regina asked her what the doctor had said about my leg. The nurse said, "The doctor wants the infection to ripen so that he can cut it. But right now he doesn't want me to touch it. Actually he comes by our little hospital every third or fifth day. He has to look after a bigger hospital in a nearby town. The poor man is terribly overworked."

The nurse told us that in the spring this old hospital I was in would be rebuilt, to be as good as or better than it had been before the war. Then she asked Regina to have some tea with her, and she invited Omar, also. They all went to have tea, and I walked into the washroom next to the entrance door. There were sinks, but no running water, only two pails and both of them only half full. Several towels were hanging there, and there was a piece of soap on one of the sinks. I took some water, undressed, and washed myself. After putting the clean new pants on, I went slowly to my bed and lay down.

As I lay there resting, Omar and Regina came in to say goodbye. Regina said that as soon as they cut the swollen, sore part of my right calf open, all the pus would come out, and there wouldn't be any more pain. The same would happen with my left leg. I had known all this before, but when Regina said it, it made me feel better. Omar just shook my hand and said that if he could get permission in two weeks he would come visit me again.

"Take care," I said. "Don't you start dreaming at work in the mine. See what it got me."

Then they left me. I was alone again. Most of the Russian patients had broken legs or broken bones. They all gave me the impression that they were content to be able to sleep, rest, and eat, without having to get up early and go to work.

I had brought my padded pants and my windbreaker as well as my mine shirt and pants, and I put them all under the bed; whenever the old woman swept the floor, I told her to leave them there, because I would need them soon to go to the toilet. Actually I only used the padded pants and the windbreaker, but I didn't want her to take my mine clothes away.

The swelling continued. It went all the way down to the ankle. The doctor stopped by again during his rounds to look at my legs. He felt them—not too tenderly—and then said to the nurse:

"In a few days when I come back we'll open it up."

On his way out he must have said something else to the nurse, because half an hour or so later she returned alone and put a wet towel with snow wrapped inside it on my right calf. It relieved the burning hot pain for a while.

From then on, on my daily trips to urinate I always brought back some snow with me inside the towel the nurse had given me. By concentrating and restraining myself, I only had to go out once during the day and once during the night. Before, I had had to go out twice during the day and once at night. I drank less water in the washroom, although I was burning with thirst. I knew the more I drank the more I would have to go outside.

My right leg was becoming heavier and heavier. I couldn't even wiggle my toes without feeling stabs of pain. The color of my leg was a shining, glistening red, and the skin was as tight as a drum. To control myself from screaming took such effort that, at times, I wished I had a knife to open it up myself. And it was still growing. My left leg continued swelling also, but it was only about half the size of the right.

During the long evenings, the other patients chattered away and swapped stories. They asked me a few times to join them, but I told them that I couldn't for my legs were hurting too much.

A few days before Christmas, it was snowing. The other patients were complaining about being cold, especially at the night. I wasn't so aware of it because whenever I went outside I had to walk slowly and I was so cold by the time I had finished that when I entered the room again it felt cozy and warm. The stove in the ward was kept burning twenty-four hours a day by the old woman who swept the floor and took the empty soup plates away. She also brought two fresh pails of water to our washroom every day.

Conditions were much better than at the camp, and best of all, there were no guards. If I hadn't been in such pain, it would have felt like a vacation. But the agony had increased to the point where I was delirious. Now the trips outside lasted at least an hour. Outside, I screamed with tears and curses. Inside the ward I cried with dry sobs and gnashing teeth. I couldn't let anyone see me cry. Crying was a sign of weakness.

In the evening the pain was at its worst, eating me up, burning my insides out. I looked at my right ankle and realized that the color was a darker red than it had been before. I wondered how it had managed to grow so much. It looked larger than my waist. I stared at it, fascinated. I became cold and then hot, but I kept staring at my ankle. Just above the joint of the ankle I saw something like a blister growing, but I couldn't understand what it was. I stared at it harder than before. It was slowly growing larger. I thought I was going crazy. Involuntarily my big toe twitched, and the blister slowly burst open. Then I twitched my big toe again, and the pus came gushing out. It was a yellow, greenish-blue color and smelled putrid. The pressure eased, but I still stared at my leg unbelievingly.

A nurse appeared from nowhere and brought a pan. She placed my leg on it so that the escaping pus wouldn't completely dirty the bed. It seemed to run for a long time. It was still running when the nurse came and brought another pan and took the first one away. I heard some people complaining about the smell. I just kept on staring. I could hardly believe that the pressure was off my leg and the intense pain was gone. The swelling seemed to shrink before my eyes. What a relief it was!

The other leg opened up too, at the shin about halfway between the foot and the knee. That happened at midnight, after the nurse had inserted some cotton into the opening in the right leg and bandaged it up. There was a lot less pus in the left leg than in the right. After it had stopped running, the nurse inserted some cotton into that opening, too, and then she left for the night. I lay there alone, completely drained of energy. But at last I could think clearly again.

Chapter XVI

THE SECOND DAY after my legs had burst, the doctor came around again. He seemed to be satisfied with my condition, and he expected that in a week or so all the pus would be gone and my legs would start to heal. In another three weeks I would be well enough to be sent back to Mine 28. He sounded very optimistic. After he left, I went slowly to the toilet. I still felt the pain as I walked, but it was an easy journey in comparison with the countless slow, painful ones I had made. I went up to the next floor; the stairs, however, gave me a lot of trouble and pain, so from then on I went outside as usual.

And so the days went on. On the inside of my right calf a hole opened up and pus came out of it, not a lot, but it ran constantly. The hole seemed to get wider, as if something was eating it from the inside. The same thing happened to the original opening at my ankle. After a few days I had two more openings on my leg.

I began to worry about these openings with the pus constantly ooz-
ing out of them. The same thing happened with my left leg. Two more
holes opened up there. They were all very ugly sores, and they continued to widen. When the nurses changed the bandages, I noticed that
they had perplexed frowns on their faces. They too didn't know what it
meant.

A day or so later the doctor appeared again, and when he saw my
legs he grumbled, looked at the sores, and then smelled them. I heard
him say something to the nurses about amputation. I froze inside. He
left, saying that the next time he stopped by he would bring along the
necessary instruments and they would see then.

My legs to be *amputated!* I had to think quickly.

For the first time in a month, I thought about escaping. In some
ways the chances were better than from the camp. The hospital was in
Rovenki, which had a huge coal yard. All the coal from the surrounding
mines was shipped went from here. In the winter the trains and the train
yards weren't so heavily guarded.

I don't think I slept at all during the next forty-eight hours. I
weighed the chances between an escape in the middle of winter without
food or sufficient clothing against the strong possibility of my legs being
amputated. I decided to escape.

Two days after the doctor's visit, in the late evening when everybody
was asleep, I went to the washroom with all my clothes. I stole a cap and
some wire, which the miners used to wrap their footrags and pants, from
the clothes on the wall near the entrance of the ward. In the washroom
I wrapped the bandages as tight as I could, and then I took a towel, slowly ripped it in half, and wrapped my feet in the two pieces. I wound the
wire about the footrags and the bottom of my pants. Then I put on my

mine pants and wrapped them with wire, too. Finally I put on my padded heavy pants, shirt, windbreaker, cap, and galoshes, and went out. I didn't look back. It was a bright, moonlit night. I slowly walked past the few dimly lit windows of the hospital and then I increased my pace.

I saw an old man and asked him if I was going in the right direction for the train station. He grumbled, "Yes, next street, turn right—a few minutes away." Behind the station there was a huge yard, and trains were maneuvering around. I spotted a train loaded with coal. There were a few Russians in sight, but they were busy switching a train to another track. Quickly I climbed up onto one of the low open cars. The steam was still rising from the coal. It probably hadn't left the bowels of the Donbas more than twenty-four hours ago.

I found a spot where the coal was like grave dust, and I started to dig a hole for myself so that I would be somewhat protected from the cold. The train moved backward and forward for a while, and then it stood still for about half an hour. Finally it began to roll.

I could see from the stars that we were going west. I cuddled into my windbreaker as snugly as I could and began to drowse off, listening to the noise the wheel below me made as it hit the joint where one rail joined the next. The train speeded up, and these clicks became more frequent. Every time the wheel hit a joint, I was one rail length farther from Mine 28 and the hospital.

This was the only way to escape from the Donbas. That was what I had decided a year ago. My biggest problem was that I didn't even have a loaf of bread with me. I knew that eventually I would have to find some way to get food when the train stopped for water. However, I wanted to be out of the Donbas at least a day before I attempted anything. I figured that there would be no more prison camps around by that time. No one would think that a prisoner would try to escape during the winter, anyhow. I would find a way to get food, I had to—there was no way back, now. The pain in my right leg was only slight, and my left leg was practically pain-free.

I allowed myself a rare luxury—I thought of my mother. I spoke to her and kept saying, "I'm rolling home—coming closer to you every moment." I looked at the sky. The millions of stars were as hard and bright as diamonds. An occasional *poroda* hill stuck out of the white blanket that surrounded me and sent out gusts of warm air.

I was very uncomfortable and twice as cold as I had been in camp. As I shivered, I thought that there wasn't another warm place left on this earth. But at least the cold overpowered the hunger I felt. Fortunately, I had the Russian cap that I had stolen, and I tied down the earflaps to keep my cheeks well protected.

It must have been around noon when the train slowed down. I looked around me, but didn't see any town or village, only a water tower and a nearby shack. There was no one in sight, but smoke was coming out of the thin chimney. All of a sudden, I knew that I would get something to eat at the shack if I tried. I just knew it!

The train slowed down and finally stopped under the tower. I rolled to the edge of the coal car and dropped down in the snow. But when I landed on the ground my legs collapsed. The circulation had stopped completely, or so it seemed. I remained there in the snow, lying on my back. I moved my legs a little until they obeyed orders again. Then I walked to the shack. I looked in through a small window and saw that no one was inside. I knocked on the door, and there was no answer. I tried it and found that it was open.

I walked right in and immediately began to search for food. I found myself half a loaf of bread and a pot full of cold kasha. The stove was red-hot with glowing coals inside. As I felt the first wave of warmth from the stove, I wanted to crawl into it, it seemed so warm and friendly. I gulped down the kasha, put the bread in a piece of *Pravda* newspaper I found, and left. I knew which car I had been in and climbed up. I settled into my hollow and started to devour the bread. I had been lucky. The door of the shack could have been locked, or the workers might have been there.

About ten minutes later the train started off again. After I finished the bread I was thirsty, so I ate some clean snow from the edge of the car. I looked at the piece of *Pravda* I had wrapped the bread in. I couldn't read too well because of the moving train, but I saw something about the Soviet and American sectors of Germany. Then down in the corner of the paper I saw a small headline about Communist Romania.

That started me thinking. What was I escaping to? If Romania was under a Communist regime, and they knew my name and birthplace and that I had escaped from Russia, then I could be arrested again and brought right back to Mine 28.

If I was lucky, I would be able to get something to eat tomorrow the way I had today, but it was very unlikely. In another day or so this train would have to cross the huge Dnieper River. After that, I would have to decide whether to get on a train going southwest toward the Romanian border or on one going northwest to Poland and from there to Germany.

Months ago Omar and I had overheard some Russians talking about a divided Germany, but we hadn't paid too much attention. Now I had to think about it seriously. The canned food I had seen in the past labeled "PORK SAUSAGE, U.S.A." seemed like something out of a fairy tale. If America had so much food that they sent thousands of cans of it to the Donbas, what would it be like, I wondered, to live in such a country? Although I wanted badly to see my mother, my father, my home, I decided right then that I could not face the danger of being arrested again. When I thought of the two and a half years behind me, I knew that I would go anywhere, just as long as it was far away from the long arm of the sickle. I decided to try for Poland, and then for Germany, where I would enter the American sector.

It wasn't quite so cold any more, although the wind was still powerful. Snowflakes started dancing down from the gray sky, and I dozed off into a disturbed half-sleep.

When I came out of it, I realized that the train was standing still. I couldn't tell whether it was dawn or twilight. I was covered with snow. My legs were completely stiff and it took a while before I could move them. I got out of my hole, rolled to the edge of the car, and dropped to the ground. It was getting lighter, so it must be morning. The cold didn't cause me as much discomfort as it should have, and that alarmed me. I wasn't far from freezing to death.

There were several shacks with smoke rising from their chimneys, and not far beyond them was a small village. I got up off the ground and stumbled toward the shacks. The second looked like a blacksmith's shop, because I saw crowbars, hammers, and a wheelbarrow next to the entrance. The door was shut, but not locked, and I went right in. It was a smithy, just as I had guessed. The stove was glowing, and I went over to it, forgetting about everything else. What a delight it was to feel such warmth again! After a while, I just lay down on the floor and fell asleep.

Chapter XVII

WHEN I AWOKE, two Russians were leaning over me. From the questioning looks on their faces I knew that they wanted an explanation: who was I and what was I doing there?

I sat up, wondering what I should tell them. The best chance I had was to arouse their pity. I started telling them that I was a Romanian who had been a very good worker in the Donbas. But a mine cave-in had injured my legs, and the doctors, instead of trying to save them, were going to amputate. I said that if someone my age lost his legs, it would make him a pretty useless worker, and I had decided to save them myself.

They pondered this story awhile and then asked to see my legs. I untied my mine pants and then the white pants from the hospital and started to unwrap the bandages. While I was doing this, I forgot that my legs would be in a terrible condition. The sight of the pus-soaked bandages was unbelievable, and the smell was repulsive. It didn't smell too bad to me, because I was used to it, but they were not. They looked at me, and I saw nothing but pity in their eyes. One of them left and came back with some clean rags, saying:

"Here, take these and use them for your legs."

Then the other one said, "If you want, we can give you some food, and for two days you can rest here. But no longer than that. In that time you can easily catch another train going west. We have no other place for you to rest besides the blacksmith shop. You can stay here, but you mustn't speak to anyone, or else the police or the authorities will find out that we helped you."

That blacksmith shop seemed like a luxurious hotel. I will wish as long as I live that I might someday be able to repay those kind people for their help. I know that they had little food, but they gave me several hot plates of good soup to eat while I was there and some cornbread.

I washed my bandages and dried them over the ever-glowing fire. I never left the fireside for a moment, and yet I couldn't stop shivering. I found out that I was only a few hours from the Dnieper. That made me feel good. At this rate I could get to West Germany within another three weeks.

The next day I caught a train. The blacksmith told me that he was pretty sure it was going northwest. He advised me to wait for the next one, which was going southwest to the Romanian border, but I decided against this. I had already made up my mind to stay away from home. It hadn't been easy, but it had to be done.

I found a car, but it was much more difficult to dig myself in, because the coal was already half frozen. Still I managed somehow, and shortly the train was underway, rolling toward the west—farther and farther away from the Donbas.

The day I had spent huddling by the glowing stove in the black-smith's shop had revived me, but another day and night on the train and I would again reach the point where the pain from my legs would grow less because of the freezing temperature. That was the danger point. I had to get off the train then, or the numbness from the cold would make me drowsy and I would freeze to death.

I began to wonder how I would find a doctor—even more, whether he would be able to heal my legs, for the sores were now a dark green, and they were constantly growing. Even if I escaped, they might ampu-tate my legs. The cold was draining all my strength. I felt there was nothing left but the naked, inexorable will to escape with both my legs attached to my body.

Time passed. The train rolled on. It became darker. I struggled to raise myself a little. The giant river Dnieper stretched out in front of the speeding train. On both sides of the bridge were little houses all lit up. Sitting up, I would certainly be seen by the bridge guards, so I ducked back into my hole. A few moments later I knew we were crossing the river from the hollow sound the train made. The Donbas was now far behind me.

Close by the bridge was a town and a train yard. As the train slowed down, I peered from my hiding place. It was a very busy yard. Train workers were bustling around like mad. I decided that if the train remained there until it was dark, I would leave the car. But after a few minutes the train started up again, and there was nothing I could do but hope it would stop before I froze to death.

At times I was tortured by doubts, because I didn't know for sure that the train I was riding on was going toward Poland. It might very well turn and go to one of the cities directly north. They needed coal as much as the Red-occupied territory. But the stars promised that we were still going northwest.

I was afraid to doze. I might never wake up again. It had grown dark long ago. The train just had to stop soon. I felt I didn't have much life left in me. It began to snow again. No stars were glittering, no moon, just icy whipping wind and whirling snowflakes. I kept fighting the comforting drowsy iciness. There didn't seem to be any pain left at all. I pulled my hand out of my windbreaker and raised it, hoping that the icy wind hitting it would wake me up. But it took too much effort to keep it up, so I pulled it back into the arm of the windbreaker to keep it as warm as possible. I started counting to keep myself awake. *Odin...dva...tre...cetere...piat...*I counted and counted and got lost in the numbers.

I must have dozed off into the comfortable coldness. With a start I awoke and realized that the train was standing still. I tried to move out of my dugout, but I was too stiff. I saw several shacks. The darkness was slowly giving way to daylight. I must have been riding the entire night.

Then the train began to move. If I didn't get off now, I would be a frozen corpse within a few hours. So I half rolled, half jumped, off and landed on a pile of snow.

I lay there without moving. The noise of the train grew fainter and fainter until it disappeared. When I raised my head, the first thing I saw was smoke rising out of one of the chimneys. Getting up on my feet was a task in itself. I staggered like a drunk toward the shack. As I got to the door, it opened and an old man came out. When he saw me, he stopped, stroked his beard, and called to someone in the shack, "Andrei, come on here."

Andrei, another old man, came out, and when he saw me he said, "What is this? Who are you?" By this time I was thinking fast. I decided the best thing to do was to tell them the truth, as I had at the smithy.

"I will tell you everything, but I am practically frozen. Let me come inside."

Andrei nodded agreement and we went inside. The glowing stove made the coal from the Donbas seem wonderful.

I told them my story. They agreed to let me stay for a few days. During the day they worked for the railway line as section hands. Pyotr, the man who had come out first, said he wanted me to do something for him while they were working.

"It is dark when we leave, and dark when we come back," he said. "My eyes are bad, and by our poor lamp I can't see very well." He showed me a fairly new windbreaker with a large rip in the back. "You are young, and you have good eyes. While you rest here, maybe you can sew this for me."

It seemed incredible. Not long ago I had feared freezing to death, and now I was offered a warm shack for several days, provided I did some tailoring. I even forgot my legs for the moment. They warmed some soup and offered me a plate. They each ate a plateful. They had a long day's work ahead of them, and they left. Before they went, they showed me some potatoes and told me to peel half of them. Toward evening, I was to start cutting them and put them on to boil.

After the Russians left, I saw some soap and a washbasin near the door. I filled a large bowl with snow outside and set it on the glowing stove. I started to unwrap my legs, the right one first. Immediately it started to hurt. As I unwrapped the calf, I saw several lice in the bandages. They seemed lazy, satiated, and content. I must have picked them up at the blacksmith's shop. To my surprise, I hadn't felt any pain from them. I picked them out and let them fall on the glowing iron plate of the stove. They crackled.

Before I did anything else, I washed my legs. The warm water felt good on the sores, but as soon as I put soap on them it burned. I cleaned my legs as well as I could without it, washed the bandages, and hung them on a line above the stove where they would dry very fast. Then I just sat in front of the stove and enjoyed the warmth. Pyotr's torn windbreaker was next. I sewed it as well as I could, and when I had finished I put the dry bandages on my legs again. Then I spread a blanket in front of the stove and lay down. I fell asleep and woke up just as it was beginning to grow dark.

There was a covered pot on the stove. I saw that it was a dark tea and poured myself some. It tasted very strong, even though it was sweetened with honey. I hadn't let myself think about food, for fear that by the time the two old fellows came back there would be nothing left. They had a bag half full of big potatoes, and I saw some barley, from which they probably made soup or kasha. In a small barrel they had some salted pork. Oh yes, there was food all around! But I could not betray their trust. They had told me not to go out of doors, for there was a village nearby and I might be seen. I felt at ease, for if they hadn't returned by now with guards, they had no intention of doing it.

The potatoes were boiling when the two men returned. They were both cursing, but when they entered the shack, they stopped and looked around. I had also cleaned up a little. They smiled, grunting approval. Pyotr took the windbreaker in his hands and examined my sewing.

"Well done," he said.

Then Andrei started to prepare the soup. He put some salt pork in it, and it turned out to be a really fine soup. We each had two platefuls, and then they gave me the rest. After supper they asked me to show them my legs, which I did.

"I have a little vodka left," Pyotr said. "You're welcome to use it if you want."

"It wouldn't do much good for my legs," I said, "and besides, it would only hurt me. I have to get medical aid soon, or I'll lose them."

It was an unpleasant subject. But then they asked me to tell them about the mine, the camp, and my home. Pyotr told me that his wife had left him when he returned home from the war wounded. But as a whole, these two old fellows seemed to be pretty content. Even taking into consideration that the front had changed several times in this area, they were relatively well off, compared to the people of the Donbas.

I found out that Kiev was already far behind me, which meant that after another day on the train I would be in Poland, or at least at the border. This was encouraging news.

I wanted to stay at the shack for as long as a week, but it would probably have been too dangerous. They asked me whether I would be comfortable enough sleeping on two empty potato bags they had, with a blanket to cover me. I answered that I would be fine.

Then Pyotr filled the stove with coal right up to the top, blew out the light, and lay down to sleep. I put the bags in front of the stove and covered myself with the blanket. We said good night, and shortly thereafter the two of them fell asleep. One of them snored lightly. Two grand old fellows!

When I woke up, I didn't know what time it was, for it was dark all around me except near the stove where the plate was glowing red-hot.

The ceiling reflected the heat, and I was perspiring. I turned my back toward the stove so that it would soak up as much warmth as possible and fell back into a deep slumber. There's nothing like a deep, dreamless sleep to make you rested and sound.

I heard a crackling noise and opened my eyes. Pyotr was putting new coal on the still glowing burned-out coal.

"Good morning," he said. "How are your legs today? Did you sleep well?"

"I slept very well, and my legs didn't pain me at all."

Andrei said, "Vanya, I will leave you this half-bagful of sunflower seeds. Roast them before we come home, and boil some potatoes again. Late tonight, I think two trains will stop here. They are both going west. You should catch one of them, because tomorrow our foreman is stopping by here with our rations. It wouldn't be good if he found you."

Then they gave me some bread, and we all had some of that sweetened tea that Pyotr made before they left. I looked out through a hazy, yellow window pane and shuddered. It was windy out, and a storm was brewing. How would the night be on the open coal car again? I just had to make it. I had to last another day and night. With these thoughts on my mind, I dozed off. But dreams, violent dreams about the camp, the black mine, and the tower in a snow blizzard woke me up again.

Still, I hadn't done badly. I was close to succeeding, which seemed impossible even to the Russians, who were used to their winters. I knew that if I could get on one of the trains tonight, I would get to the border.

When the two men came home, Andrei said, "We have good news for you. At eleven o'clock tonight a train will stop here, and it is bound for Brest-Litovsk on the border. You had better eat and warm yourself, for it's a long journey. Pyotr and I don't understand how you traveled here from the Donbas in open train cars. You must be very tough."

Then Pyotr said, "Let's make a good soup for you. You must eat well so that you have strength."

It was very touching how these two strangers were concerned about me. I had learned in the last two years that the more demanding the basic needs of self-preservation grow, the closer one comes to nature. Under extreme conditions, pretenses vanish. I was certain that if the authorities found out that Pyotr and Andrei had hidden me and given me food, there would be no leniency in their punishment, and yet they took the chance, because they felt and saw and understood.

Pyotr had an old watch, which he took out of his pocket and put on the table. In about an hour they had a fine, rich soup ready. I ate like a lord. They each had only one plateful and insisted that I finish the rest. I ate four helpings.

Before I left, Andrei gave me a satchel of roasted sunflower seeds and told me that the train should be in presently. A few minutes later we heard the train approaching. Pyotr said that I should guide myself by the tower where the engine would fill up with water. They both wished me good luck, and Pyotr said, "God be with you." We shook hands and I went outside, walking in the direction of the tower, which wasn't very far away.

The train passed me and I kept walking, guided by the light on the tower. It was a long train; the end hadn't passed yet. The engine stopped under the tower, and I headed for the low coal cars. I found one where the coal wasn't made of very big chunks, and I dug myself in. It wasn't as hard for me to do it now as it had been on the first car.

Not long after, I was on my way.

Chapter XVIII

I HAD FORTIFIED myself so strongly for this ride that I was relieved at not finding it so brutal. It wasn't as comfortable as the shack, but it wasn't as bad as my memory had painted the last night on the other train.

The train made one short stop toward morning, but started off again right away. It was just getting light, and I saw that we were leaving a fairly large town behind us. The country here seemed quite heavily populated. Whenever I looked up, which wasn't too often, I saw villages disappearing behind us or appearing in the distance. I didn't look up very often, because the cold wind would hit me in the face and make me even colder than I already was.

It was late afternoon and daylight was starting to fade when I raised my head once again and saw a large city coming into view. I knew that this had to be Brest-Litovsk.

I huddled in the coal as deep as I could. I felt like an ostrich who buries his head in the sand so the hunter can't see him, or so he thinks. Anyway, I didn't want to be seen, and I didn't want to see. I realized how far I had come and how much I had accomplished, and I was proud of myself.

The next hurdle was to cross the border without being caught. The train gradually began to decrease its speed, until it finally stopped completely. But after a minute or so it started again. They had probably had to wait for a switch to be changed. It rolled along slowly for another ten minutes or so and then came to a definite stop. I stayed quietly where I was and waited to see whether it would start moving again. But it stood still.

It was almost dark. I waited another half hour and started to get down. I couldn't see much; just some trains and a huge yard. I left the freight car and started walking alongside the train. I walked faster and faster. My circulation slowly increased and took the stiffness out of my bones.

On the right side of the yard, stretching toward the city, I saw some houses. But on the left side there were several houses, too. I walked in that direction first, hoping to find someone I could trust. As I came closer to the houses I saw that there were several trees there and that the ground sloped down in a little valley. The snow was hip-deep in places, but the path I was following had been trodden down. It took me past the first few houses and went toward the valley. Close to the bottom of the hill was a lone house with only one lighted window. I decided to try it.

I went up to the door and knocked lightly. My knock was answered by a rough voice, which was speaking not in Russian, but in Polish. I answered in Russian, saying, "Please let me in. I am a Romanian." I heard a stealthy shuffle and the door opened. It was a bald-headed man in his fifties. He beckoned for me to come in and close the door.

The room was very warm and lighted by a single dim electric bulb. He asked me:

"How the devil did you escape at this time of year?"

I said, "How did you know I escaped?"

He grunted. "The only people who would come asking for shelter in this town are people who have escaped from Russia. But only one other man, two years ago, tempted the winter. He died at the house of a fellow worker I know who had given him shelter. A German prisoner I would surely turn over to the authorities, but someone like you I will help. Please tell me where you are from and how it happened that you were a prisoner in Russia."

I interrupted and asked, "Am I not in Russia now? Is Brest-Litovsk not part of the Soviet Union?"

"No," he said, "it is Poland you are in, Poland. But the Russians do whatever they please here. So continue with your story."

I began to tell him everything that had happened to me. While I was talking, he put a pot on the stove. As it warmed he stirred it several times so that whatever was in it wouldn't burn. When I mentioned that I hadn't thought it possible to survive in the open coal cars, he just crossed himself and said:

"If you had God's help and were strong and tough enough to emerge alive from such a train ride, it is God's will that you will escape successfully." Evidently he was strongly religious. Then he told me to sit at his rough homemade table, and he put a spoon, a plate, and the pot from the stove on it.

"Eat," he said. "Eat it all, because tomorrow I will have two more rabbits in my sling traps, and I will prepare them."

He explained that even in the winter months he caught two or three rabbits every week. The Russian he spoke was completely different from the dialect they used in the Donbas, and this, along with the Polish accent, made his speech sound strange to me, but I had no trouble understanding him. He told me his name was Stanislaus.

After I finished eating, he gave me something to drink called *kvass,* which is a brown brew containing some alcohol. It tasted like a bitter, dry herb. Then he asked me to unwrap my legs and show him my wounds. By now it was nothing for me to look at the soaked bandages. He wasn't very shocked either when he saw them. He proceeded to heat some water without saying a thing. I washed the wounds and then the bandages. There were some more lice in the wounds, but I hadn't felt them.

After the bandages had dried, I put them on again and turned to him and said, "Stanislaus, how can I thank you for your help?"

He ignored my question and said, "Your problems are behind you. You won't find it too difficult to get away from our big yard here. You must already know that the gauge of the rails changes from the Eastern size to the smaller European size. Within half a day or so, you'll be in Warsaw, and ten or fifteen hours after that you'll be in the Soviet sector of Germany. You must be very careful. But since you've come so far, you will succeed with the rest of your escape."

In the morning when I woke up Stanislaus was filling the stove with coal. I wanted to get up at once and help, but I was surprised to find that my legs were very stiff and painful. Then my surprise turned to fear. What the devil could be wrong with them now? I forced myself to move despite the pain. After I had gotten up and folded my blanket, the stiffness disappeared, and the old familiar pain came in its place.

After Stanislaus went to work, I saw an old map of Europe on the far wall. I looked at it and my eyes went to Brasov, Romania. I felt tears welling up. I knew already that there would be no homecoming for me. But it was so terrible when I thought of it! From now on I would be a foreigner wherever I went. I felt so sad that I lay down and escaped into sleep.

Stanislaus woke me up. I didn't hear him come in. He just shook my shoulders gently, and when I opened my eyes, he was looking down at me.

It was almost night. I had slept through the day. The rest had restored my strength somewhat. Stanislaus was skinning a rabbit, and another one was lying on the floor. He had said that he would have two of them, and he did.

We spoke about the trains. Stanislaus said that if I could get on a train bound for the Soviet sector of Germany, I would be there in about a day. I decided to try right after dinner. Stanislaus said he would walk me to the yards. No one would be suspicious if he asked for the information.

Soon the rabbits were ready, and they tasted so good that we finished both of them. Stanislaus prayed and crossed himself before beginning his meal. He said that he usually didn't eat so much, but that seeing my appetite made him very hungry, too.

After we had finished he said, "Vanya, if I had some bread, I would offer it to you for the road."

I thanked him for all he had already given me and said:

"May God repay you."

These words seemed to please him, and together we started for the station. Only an old man who was going to fetch water passed us on the way.

When we arrived, Stanislaus told me to wait while he went to find out what he could about the trains. He returned after about half an hour, and assured me that within an hour a train would pull out of the yard heading for Warsaw. He said he didn't think it was a coal train, but I should try to get on it anyway. He shook hands with me and was gone before I could properly thank him.

When the train finally came, I could see only closed boxcars. Then several cars passed that had chimneys with smoke rising from them. They baffled me at first, but then I realized what they were. Twenty-five months ago I had entered the Donbas in a similar car. It all seemed so terribly long ago. These cars probably held German war prisoners who were being repatriated.

As the train stopped, I walked up to the closest car and saw some faces peering at me through a small window. I asked in German whether any of them knew where they were. They answered that they were somewhere in Poland. Then they asked me who I was.

"Can you open the door of your car?" I asked.

They didn't reply right away, but a quick whispering went on inside. Then someone said, "Okay, but at our next stop, which will be tomorrow, you must disappear quickly because we will be counted."

They slid the door open. I reached up and several hands grabbed mine and pulled me in. It was very dark inside, but then someone lit a tiny oil lamp. I was surrounded by haggard, drawn faces. Had they been like the prisoners in my camp, twenty voices would have been raised at once. Here only one fellow asked the questions. I had to say that I was Romanian, because he asked me whether I had lived in Germany before the war. None of them believed my age when I told them.

In the middle of the car was a coal stove, similar to the one we had had in our car two years ago. They were all cold, but they offered me a place next to the stove. I told them in my not too fluent German that I had escaped from Russia. One of the prisoners spoke Russian, and when I found this out, I continued my story in Russian and he translated for the others.

The train started. It rolled faster and faster. It seemed that once more lady luck was with me. Now and then someone refilled the stove with coal. It was almost dawn. The train was going at full speed. One of the men who was sitting by the window said, "We're coming into a large city. This is probably Warsaw, the capital of Poland."

I had to get off before the guards who were riding in the last car found me. Every door was shut with a hook from the outside, but the Germans had figured out a way to open them from the inside with a wire. That was how they had let me into the car, back in Brest. As soon as the train stopped, I could jump off. I would have to close the hook so the guards wouldn't notice that it had been open during the night. Then I would crawl under the car to the other side and get away as fast as I could.

When we got into the huge Warsaw train yard the train slowed down. We opened the door, and the moment the train stopped I jumped. My legs collapsed, and I had to force myself upright. I turned around, put the stiff iron hook into place, and crawled under the car. Then I heard a shout: "Where are you going?"

I froze inside, but didn't stop. On the other side of the train I saw another train, and another, and I kept on crawling and crawling. I must have crawled under six trains when I looked back and saw several pairs of feet standing in front of the car I had been riding in. But no one was coming after me. I got up and walked as fast as I could between the trains. The train on my right came to an end. I crossed the track and crawled under the next five or six trains, until there were no more tracks left to cross.

Beyond the station there was a factory and several large houses and buildings. I walked toward them as fast as I could. Once I had rounded a corner, I felt better. There seemed to be no commotion behind me. They had probably opened the car, counted the prisoners, and after finding everyone present, dismissed their suspicions.

As soon as my tension eased, I began to look around me. I was in a more or less busy section, and laborers were coming and going. Many of them stared at me.

Then I saw a girl who was wearing nylon stockings. I felt embarrassed looking at her legs that were bare from the feet to the knee. All the women in the Donbas wore long pants under their skirts. I followed the girl with my eyes until she disappeared into one of the buildings. I felt a longing, a desire to touch. Back home I had seen silk stockings and nylons, and my mother's and sister's underwear. It had only been underwear, nothing special. But now the sight of such flimsy material represented everything soft and womanly.

I started back toward the station, for I was just too conspicuous where I was, with my strangely cut dirty clothes. Although the majority of the people here were laborers, they were much cleaner and better dressed than I was. I walked to the far side of the station. The prisoners had been let out of the cars to move around a little and get some water.

I walked over to a large machine shop. Laborers were milling all around there. Since they were all dirty, I wasn't so obvious. I didn't speak to any of them. They might have understood Russian, but then again they might not have. At any rate, it would probably arouse suspicion. I just wanted to sit down somewhere, regardless of the cold, and rest a little. I went behind the shop and found a pile of cinders with no snow on them. They were still a little warm, and after sitting a few minutes I fell asleep.

I must have dozed for over two hours, because when I woke up it was almost evening. Across the way from the machine shop I saw a lot of people. There seemed to be a small bazaar there. Something made me turn. As I did, I noticed a boy, about fifteen years old, who looked and acted very fresh. He was advertising his sausages, bacon, and bread with a loud, screechy voice. The sausages were hanging on his arm, and he had the bacon and the loaves of bread in a large basket. I couldn't take my eyes off the food.

The daylight vanished. The crowd thinned out. The boy packed his sausages in the basket and started walking away. A devil seized me. I walked up to him. He turned as he heard me approaching, for the snow crunched under my feet. When I was right next to him, before he could open his mouth, my fist hit him in the face, and he fell backwards screaming. He scrambled up and I lunged at him, but he ran away. I bent over the basket, grabbed a sausage, a piece of bacon, and a loaf of bread and then turned and ran back into the train yard.

While I was running, I realized I must have been crazy to risk everything like that. Several people had begun to chase me. Luckily I was about two hundred yards ahead of them. Clutching the food, I crawled under several freight cars, got up, and ran some more. I saw a train starting to move. The car just in front of me had its door half open, and it seemed to be empty. I threw in the bread and meat and then jumped up and crawled in. I lay there panting, hoping that my sense of direction was correct, that the train was headed toward Germany.

We started picking up speed. I crawled around in the darkness until I found the food. No loaf of bread was ever devoured faster. It was white bread, and with the bacon and sausage it tasted better than the finest roast duck. After I had finished eating I moved toward the door, pulled it shut, and crawled back into a corner. I found a little straw to sleep on and dozed off, thinking about what a good guiding force instinct was. If I had planned to go and sock the obnoxious boy, take the food, and run for it, I could not have been more successful.

The rattling of the train acted like a sleeping pill, because when I woke up the sun was pouring through the door, which had jiggled open. We were standing still now. It was terribly cold. I had to get up very slowly. Just as I reached the door, the train jerked into motion again. I stood at the door and watched. The train yard was quite large. At the end of the station I saw a sign near the road. I couldn't read exactly what it said, but I saw "90 km." That must be the distance between the border and where we are, I thought. Then I passed another sign which said "Poznan," probably the name of the city we had just passed.

I moved my arms up and down and rubbed my hands together to get the blood circulating. Then I took my galoshes off and rubbed my feet until they got a little warmer. After closing the door, although I was miserably cold, I lay down again. The rattling of the train put me to sleep.

Next thing I knew, the train had stopped again and I was frozen stiff as a board. I heard singing outside. It sounded like a Russian army song. Then I heard marching. I staggered to the door and peeked through a crack. A large group of Russian soldiers were marching past the station. The tune reminded me of the Donbas. These soldiers must be Russian occupation troops.

The soldiers disappeared, and when I saw that no one was near my freight car, I jumped off. I saw several switches not far ahead and walked toward them. An old man with some tools was repairing something. He looked me up and down.

"*Armer Teufel* [poor devil]," he said in German.

Relief filled me. I was out of Poland!

In my broken German I told the old man my story. He scratched his head and said, "Do you think you can last another ride of several hours?"

"I'll probably freeze if I have to ride in one of those freights again," I said.

"I have a brother who is an engineer. Within the hour he is leaving with his train for Gotha. He'll let you ride in the cabin on the engine where it's warm. It's too dangerous for you to stay here any more, for this in Frankfurt-on-the-Oder. There are a lot of Russian soldiers in this city, and with your strange clothes they would probably stop you if you tried to walk anywhere." I believed him.

He told me to wait. If anyone came near the switches, he said, I should pick up a tool and look busy. He was going to find out exactly when the train was leaving, and if possible he would speak to his brother.

After he left I picked up a wrench. All the people I had met had been so kind! I saw several trains come and go, and not far off I saw a building that was probably the station. A number of workers or Russian soldiers stood about, but no one came to ask any questions. I must have looked like another worker. That's what I hoped, anyhow.

About half an hour passed, and then two men came toward me. As they drew close, I recognized the kind old German. He had brought his brother. There was no time for thanks. The brother told me to come with him. The old man offered me his hand and said *"Auf Wiedersehen, mein Freund."*

I left with his brother. We walked toward several engines standing on railroad sidings. When we got to the second one, he climbed up and motioned for me to come up, too. Inside he said, "Hey, *Junge*, crouch behind my stool." Then he turned and put the steam on. The engine moved backward faster and faster. When it stopped, he hollered something out the window. For several minutes we moved forward, and then we backed up again. Stopping jolted me, and pain shot through me from my legs.

The engineer spoke to someone through the window again, and then a man climbed up into the cabin. He sat down next to the engineer and winked at me. The locomotive had been hitched up, and we began to move. Then it stopped and Otto, the engineer, left the cab, returning a few minutes later with a package.

The ride began again. The engineer's helper, whose name was Hans, started shoveling coal into the huge furnace. When he finished, it was so nice and warm that I lay down and fell asleep. It had never occurred to me before that the need for heat might become more demanding than the need for food, but the last ten or fifteen hours I had spent in that ice-cold freight car from Warsaw made me feel that way.

It seemed hours later when Hans woke me up. Otto pulled out the package and shouted: "To eat...to eat." We had to shout to each other in order to be heard above the hissing locomotive. I crouched to the side behind the engineer's place while the assistant shoveled coal into the furnace. That was the reason he had awakened me, to stoke the furnace. I opened the package and found a thick liverwurst sandwich and a nice apple. It was good, but so little. I smelled the apple and started to take little bites out of it. It grew smaller and smaller until there was none left.

The soothing rattling and the comfortable warmth lulled me to sleep again. I awoke to discover that we were standing still. It was morning. I heard Otto talking to someone as he climbed into the engine. I could understand some words about a poor prisoner from Russia, and I knew that he was speaking about me. He entered the locomotive with another man, who had a very kind face which I liked immediately. He had bushy eyebrows and blue, blue eyes. Otto told me that this was Helmut. Helmut would take me as far as Gotha, where they both knew a doctor they had met during the war who would look at my legs. From there they would put me on a train that would take me out of the Soviet sector and into West Germany.

I said goodbye to Otto and thanked him for all he had done for me. Words were so little, but what could I do?

Helmut told me that we would have a passenger train behind us, so we would have to be on time. A little later we were on our way. Helmut also gave me a liverwurst sandwich. He tried to talk with me, but my German was very poor, and it was much too noisy. We finally had to give up. He told me with motions to lie down in front of the furnace, which I did.

Around noon our train rolled into Gotha. As soon as it stopped, Helmut wrote a short letter, which he handed to me. He took me out of the train yard to a street and told a young boy passing by to take me to a certain street. He gave me some silver coins, looked me in the eye as a father does before his son leaves for military service, shook my hand, and walked off.

The boy looked at me as if I had come from another world. I would have like to know what he was thinking. Whenever I caught his eyes as we walked, he always looked away first. He was probably embarrassed by my misery. Who knows? We went first to the left, then to the right, and then the boy pointed to a sign that said "Optician."

I rang twice before an elderly woman peeked through the door. She shut it quickly, but I said, *"Brief. Ich hab' einen Brief."*

She thrust her hand out, and I gave her the letter that Helmut had given me. Soon the door was opened by a man of about sixty or seventy. He stood there and stared for a moment, and then motioned me inside.

We went through a nice living room and into the study. The doctor asked me to show him my legs, and I started to unwrap the bandages. I had never seen the wounds look so bad. The doctor heated some water and washed them. He threw away all the old bandages, which were a sight, but I wanted to wash them and keep them, because I had come to believe that without those bandages I wouldn't be able to take another step. The doctor said that he was going to give me a newly developed medicine. He took a red tablet from a vial on his shelf and scraped off some powder, which he put on my wounds. Then he took out several clean gauze bandages. How white they were!

While he worked, he asked me about the conditions in the camp, and whether I had left someone behind there. As I told him about Omar, I couldn't keep back my tears.

"Yes," I said, "I have someone back there who saved my life. He was a real friend."

Then I couldn't talk any more, or I would have broken down completely. There were so many cold, bitter things stored up in me. I was beginning to feel angry at all that had happened to me, but then I thought that not many people encountered as much human dignity and kindness as I had during my escape.

The doctor put the clean, new bandages on my legs, but they felt too loose. I asked to go to the toilet, and there I unwrapped the bandages and rewrapped them much tighter. They had to be able to stand the traveling I still had ahead of me.

Then the doctor said, "I must go and check whether there is a train that is going across the border into West Germany tonight. I know several engineers who may be able to help you." He explained that once I was across the border, I would find camps in West Germany set up to feed, clothe, and take proper care of people like myself.

Before he left, he sat me down at a table in his study. The old woman who had opened the door when I first arrived brought me some hot soup and sandwiches, which I started to eat. I was very much aware of my filthy clothes, for wherever I sat and whatever I touched, I left a black imprint. The doctor had told me several times to ignore that, for nothing could be done about it.

The old woman kept bringing in food. She seemed to be afraid of me, or was she shy? I saw her smile a little once, but as soon as I smiled back she busied herself with something and walked out of the room. The food in Germany must have been as scarce as it was in Russia. I could sense that from the way it was being given. After all, they had just lost a war.

The grand old doctor returned and grunted with pleasure.

"*Mein Sohn,*" he said, "tonight you will be on a train crossing over into West Germany. I spoke to an engineer I know who is taking a train there tonight. He never does such things, but as a favor to a good friend like me he will. I will walk with you to the train later, and we will meet him there."

The red powder that he had put on my legs seemed to have relieved the pain a little. As he smoked his pipe, he told me that Germany would have to go through a tough ten years before it would be able to get back on its feet again. He told me how little food the people received with their ration cards, but that I shouldn't feel bad about what I had eaten, because as a doctor he could make it up. I didn't know exactly what he meant, but I guessed that he had some patients who were farmers and brought him things from the land in payment for his services.

We passed several hours talking like that. Then, after we drank some sweetened tea, we left for the station. The old woman gave me a furtive handshake. Outside, the doctor told me that she was a sister of his, and that her nerves were very bad because of the bombings she had gone through.

We walked slowly to the train yards. It had begun to grow dark. When we reached the train yards we waited for a while. The doctor looked at his watch and said his friend should have been here by now. A few minutes later the man arrived. His name was Franz. The doctor told him to take care of me and if possible to get me a ride as far as he could toward Hannover. Then the doctor shook my hand and said that I should write and tell him how I was. He gave me his address on a piece of paper. We shook hands again, and I thanked him several times, and then he left.

Franz put his hand on my shoulder and said, "I'll hide you in the engine now, but you'll have to be quiet. I'll go and see if I can get a few potatoes. We can bake them on a rack inside the furnace, and you'll see how good they will taste."

He took me to the steaming engine, where I crouched down behind his seat, and he left. In ten minutes he came back, his pockets bulging. He had about twelve big potatoes, which he told me he had stolen from a Russian truck.

Soon we were on our way, and the silent Fritz, his assistant, took the potatoes out of the furnace. He gave me five of them and kept the rest for Franz and himself. The train slowed down and finally stopped. I was still enjoying the baked potatoes when Franz said that I would have to hide while they stopped at Eisenbach to load coal. I did hide, but it was no time at all before we were rolling again. I lay down in front of the furnace and fell asleep.

An abrupt stop woke me up. Fritz put his finger on his mouth as a signal to be absolutely quiet and motioned for me to hide. I crawled toward the hole from where the coal was shoveled. Franz turned around in his seat and urgently motioned me back through the hole leading to the coal reservoir. Not a moment too soon. Crouched in the coal, I heard a harsh Russian voice speaking in broken German, asking how they were. This was the border!

The sound of heavy steps told me that the guard had climbed into the engine. I was hardly breathing. Walking around, he swore in Russian and called the Germans "Turks." Then he climbed down and left.

I heard Franz whisper through the hole *"Noch fünf Minuten,"* and something else I didn't understand. He meant that I should wait there another five minutes. It seemed like an hour. Finally the train jerked and started to move. When I crawled out into the engine, Fritz winked at me and shook my hand.

Franz turned around and motioned for me to come to him. Shaking his head, he said that he would never again do this for anyone. It was far too dangerous. If he got caught he would lose his job. He yelled all this so that I could hear him over the hissing of the engine.

I sat back near the furnace. It was a few minutes before I really understood I was free. We had crossed the border. My escape was over. I was beyond the reach of the Donbas.

Book III

Chapter XIX

AND THAT WAS how I entered the Western world. In Kassel Franz suggested that I go into the warm waiting room of the station. There I could ask the station police where the closest camp for refugees was.

When I got off the locomotive, in spite of my eternal hunger and the miserable pain in my legs, I felt a surge of elation. I no longer had to wonder whether there was someone behind me, watching me, guards or soldiers or police. The last two and a half years had sharpened my senses so that it was as if I had an eye in the back of my head.

I found the waiting room, which was terribly crowded. The people stood in groups and talked. Some of them looked at everyone who approached their particular group with suspicion.

Finally I found a spot on a bench where I could sit down. My clothes stank, and my neighbors on the bench shifted away from me. After half an hour I was very uncomfortable. People were talking about me, but they spoke so fast in their strange dialect that I couldn't understand. But I did know that the things they were saying weren't nice. They themselves were by no means well dressed. Although my nose had been exposed to a lot of foul things in my years at the camp, it was still able to tell me that these people weren't clean. But they treated me like an outcast.

This uncomfortable situation didn't last long, for two policemen sauntering through the station stopped not far from the corner where I was sitting. They saw the crowd staring and came over slowly. I got up and met them halfway. They asked me for identification, and I couldn't help laughing. How in the world, I thought could I even start to tell them my story?

I said that I hadn't had identification for years, and that I had just escaped from the Soviet Union. It took them what seemed like a long time to understand what I was trying to tell them. Then they asked me what nationality I was. When I told them that I was Romanian, they asked me whether I spoke Hungarian. I said that I did, and one of them left immediately and returned with one of the station officials. He spoke Hungarian very well, and I started to tell him where I had come from and what had happened to me. But as he translated, the policemen continued to regard me suspiciously.

Finally they took me out of the station, but refused to say where we were going. They walked too fast, and I asked them to slow down so I could keep up with them. One of them started to take my arm, but at the last second decided against it. I knew that he had changed his mind because I was too dirty for him to touch. He said that I should walk fast because it was cold. *This,* cold? Now I stared at *him.*

Not far from the station was a Red Cross center, and they took me in there. It was a lot cleaner than the waiting room. They spoke to a woman and then said that they would leave me for a while; someone would come back for me later. The woman to whom the two policemen had spoken turned to me after they had left and asked me to sit down on a bench. She sat beside me and asked who I was, where I was from, how I had arrived here, and how old I was. She was a kind lady who had a lot of patience listening to my guttural, broken German.

Then I started to show her my two bandaged legs. As I lifted my pants she caught a whiff of the pus-soaked bandages. The sight alone was enough. She shook her head and said, "Please don't unwrap them here. This is not a first-aid room."

The poor woman. As miserable as I was, I felt sorry for her at that moment. Then she asked me whether I was hungry.

"Yes, Madame," I said, "I am very, very hungry and very, very tired."

"I'll see what I can do for you," she said.

I sat there and waited and waited. Perhaps the police and the Red Cross were battling it out over me. I was exhausted and my legs were aching. I must have drowsed off for a few minutes, but a touch on my shoulder woke me. The two policemen were standing in front of me, and the woman was talking to them. One of her hands was resting on my shoulder. I could only understand a word here and there.

When the police left, she told me to follow her. She took me into a first-aid room where an older nurse told me to show her my legs. I unwrapped them silently, and then she made me sit on a bench while she bent down to look at them. I could see that she was frightened. She murmured something and shook her head while she put some kind of cream on the wounds and started wrapping them with snow-white, new bandages. To my dismay, she wrapped them much too loosely, but I was too tired to argue with her. It was silly. They were fools. How could a man walk around without the bandages sliding down? Then my pants would rub the open wounds and inflame the raw flesh.

When I had put my pants on again the nurse took me out into an office where the other woman was on the telephone. She told me to sit down for a while. The few steps I had taken had already caused the bandages to slide down. Another hundred yards or so of walking and the wounds would be completely exposed.

She was arguing with someone over the phone. After she finally hung up, she said, "I will give you some travel rations. After you eat supper here, we will put you on a train and you will go to a fine refugee camp where they will take care of you. Maybe we can find another coat or jacket for you here, also. *Komm, Junge.*"

She took me into a small mess hall. Maybe it wasn't a Red Cross station I was in. But I remembered seeing a sign outside and a Red Cross painted on a poster somewhere. I was too confused to think about anything. I was given some soup with brown bread, some boiled potatoes, and spinach, which tasted fine, but it was so little, such small portions. While I ate, the woman drank a cup of tea. I was conscious of her eyes on me. I devoured the food as soon as it was put in front of me. I couldn't stop the compulsion to eat, faster and faster, before someone took it from me. Once the food is in the stomach, it is safe and no one can take it away.

As I was wiping my mouth I looked up. The woman was shaking her head. She was nice in a way, but too distant. Perhaps it was just the language barrier. She said that my train would leave in seven hours and that she would give me a cot to sleep on until it was time to go.

She took me to a room where a lot of clothes were lying around, mostly jackets. I had to take my filthy jacket off, and the shirt I had on underneath was torn and very dirty. The front of it, where I had gotten the two cuts in my chest from the sharp *poroda* rocks, was also crusted with blood and pus. The cuts themselves still oozed pus. After trying on nearly every jacket, we found one that was only a little short. It would have to do. The old jacket I had arrived in was as black and as filthy as my hands. Now at least I had a clean jacket. The woman asked me to throw my old one into a barrel that was used for garbage. I felt as though she was asking me to throw away an old friend.

Then she showed me to a room where several men were sleeping. The cot nearest to the door was empty, and she said:

"Take this one. Next door is the toilet. Someone will wake you up and take you to the train in time. Sleep well."

As she left I repeated *Danke* to her several times, which she acknowledged with a nod of her head before she walked out.

I went to the toilet and was amazed at the white towels. I saw a mirror and dared to look into it. I hadn't changed much, except that I was much more worn and skinny. I took off my Russian cap and saw that I had a flock of wild, dirty hair. My face alone was enough to make anyone on the street suspicious. The skin had been hardened by the wind and cold. Since I hadn't started shaving yet, there was some white fuzz on my cheeks and jaw. I had shadows under my eyes, and dirt was in every crease of my skin. Although I hadn't noticed them before, there were several frown lines on my forehead.

A small piece of soap was lying there, but it was terrible—*ersatz,* or substitute. Even the soap we had had in Russia, when we had any, was better than this. I tried to wash my hands and face, but after scrubbing and scrubbing with cold water I finally gave up and went to my soft bunk and fell asleep with my clothes and galoshes on.

Someone said, *"Auf, auf!"* and I knew that I would have to catch a
train to some camp where they were supposed to take care of me. I
hoped that I wouldn't have to go through my whole story again.

The man who had awakened me had a Red Cross on his arm. He
rushed me, and I walked as fast as I could. After a few minutes the bandages on my legs began slipping slowly down. The new jacket I had on
wasn't as warm as the windbreaker I had thrown away. My galoshes were
in very poor shape. I knew I would have a lot of trouble, no matter
where I went, finding my size.

We arrived at the station. I had thought it would be deserted, as it
was only about six o'clock in the morning. But despite the early hour,
crowds of people were already moving about. Where the devil could
they all be going? The fellow who had brought me to the station pulled
at my arm. *"Komm, Komm,"* he said, and put me on an already very
crowded train.

"Here, give this ticket to the *Schaffner,"* he said.

I didn't understand what he meant. He scratched his head and said,
"Conductor." Then I understood. He shook my hand and left.

After a sudden jerk and then another, the train was in motion. I held
an envelope in my hand. Inside I found a ticket to Hannover and an
authorized pass. This train was much better than the trains I had seen in
the past two years. The only problem was that it was terribly crowded.
But after only twenty minutes or so, the people had all moved away
from me. My dirty pants and my wounds stank. I became conscious of
it all of a sudden.

I had some ration cards that I was supposed to present to the
refugee camp where I was heading. It was all so confusing—strange
country, strange people. I had to think about what I had escaped from

to feel better. Somehow I just knew that there were thousands of questions ahead of me, mountains of questions. I would have to shovel through them like the thousands of tons of *poroda* I had shoveled in the Donbas.

I sat down on the floor and let the people stare at me. I rolled up my pants and looked at my legs. I should have wrapped the bandages more tightly myself after that stupid nurse had left. Now my wounds were bleeding and hurt terribly. I started redoing the bandages, but I was unable to finish, for the conductor and several other people had to step over me to get by. I had been concentrating so hard on what I was doing that when I looked up and saw a military uniform, a wave of fear swept through me. He was following the conductor and stopped to ask me what was wrong with my legs. He spoke in German, but it wasn't his own tongue. He was an officer, but a foreigner. I thought he must be English. I tried to tell him who I was. When I took out my papers from the Red Cross, he asked me to come with him. I wrapped my legs as fast as I could and followed him.

After passing through several cars, we came to one guarded by two soldiers. He spoke to them, and we went in. The car was empty and was carpeted like a palace. He led the way to a compartment with soft chairs and told me to sit down. I said that I didn't want to because my pants were very dirty. He looked at them, said that they were Russian pants, and told me to sit down anyway. Then he asked me what nationality I was and how I came to be on this train. I tried very hard to explain, but it was difficult because I didn't speak German well enough. He asked me for my address back home and handed me a sheet of paper and a pencil. What if I had forgotten how to write? I tried and found that I still could. He said he would do something for me if what I had told him was true. Then he offered me a cigarette, which I refused since I had never smoked, and nothing more was said.

The train rolled on, and I sat back and watched the landscape flying past our window. I thought about the other trains I had been on in the last month. What a difference! The warmth of the closed compartment felt good, but it made my legs smell even more. I was ashamed. There wasn't even any point in going to the toilet and washing my hands and face. It had taken me two years to get as dirty as I was; it would take weeks to get really clean again.

My thoughts went back to my childhood when I had ridden with my mother and father in a similar comfortable, first-class compartment. I always sat opposite my father next to the window so that he could answer any questions I had. And I always had a lot of them. Those days I took all that comfort and well-being for granted. I kept on reminiscing until I fell asleep, sitting opposite the immaculate officer.

I was in a railway car with Lisa. She was concerned about my legs. I was going to ask her how she had found me, for we weren't in the Donbas. It seemed to me that I had seen a NO SMOKING sign a few minutes ago on the wall of our car. It was a French sign, DEFENSE DE FUMER. So we couldn't possibly be in the Donbas, for we were either in France or Romania. But it was dark, and the rattling of the wheels resembled the rattling of the little cars in the levels of Mine 28. Then I realized that I was sitting with Lisa in a cart on a pile of straw. The straw was being taken to the stables where the poor blind horses rested when they weren't pulling the cars. My thoughts were shocked and confused. Hadn't I gone through terrible ordeals to escape? How was I in the mine again? I cried and cried.

"Lisa," I said, "Lisa, how am I gong to escape again and take you with me to my home? It is so hard. But first we must get out of the mine."

Then the train slowed down, and a mine lamp hung in front of it. By the dim, flickering light, I saw the braces above us. I was fascinated by the gray-black poroda *I saw between the close-spaced braces and awed by the formidable weight those braces supported.*

We were nearly at the stable when we heard voices. I recognized the young, fanatical officer who had been in charge of our camp for a month. He asked for straw, and the voice of the guard who had nearly killed me answered him, saying that the straw must be in this car that had just arrived. "But where is Lisa?" he asked. Then I heard two or three steps coming toward the car. And then silence. I was afraid to breathe for fear the straw Lisa and I were sitting on would make a noise. She was clinging to me with fright.

A vein in the mine began to crack right above me. It made a noise like tons of solid water being dropped on solid concrete. It was spine-chilling, paralyzing. Here it is, I thought, another cave-in, and I have Lisa to worry about. The two of us were trapped in the car. Lisa whispered, "My God!" The vicious guard and the officer were forgotten, and everything exploded. I clutched Lisa and screamed.

I was writhing and tearing something when I saw the frightened face of the officer at the door of the compartment. I found that during the dreadful dream I had ripped my jacket.

He realized that I had had some awful dream, but when I tried to tell him what it was about, he never really understood. How could he?

The train was still rumbling fast. Outside, the fields and forest were covered with snow.

The officer told me that we would arrive within ten minutes. I had no idea whether I was still going to Hannover or not. From what the officer said, I understood that he would send a wire to Romania to check my story. What would happen if there was no reply? Did I still have a home? I didn't even know whether my mother and father were living. Then I remembered that my mother had a brother who had left Romania when he was young and become a doctor in Germany. He had visited us once, and I had gotten along well with him. If I could find his address, perhaps he would take care of me.

All these thoughts took time to consider. Soon we arrived at a station. The officer told me to follow him, but after I had taken a few steps I realized that I had wrapped my bandages too tight. I hoped that we wouldn't have to walk far.

In the station I saw the same kind of milling crowd as in the other station. I learned later that this existed at every depot. The people were all trying to buy or sell something on the black market. As we walked past, I saw a group of people from the train following us. A dark-green bus was waiting outside. A man with a Red Cross band on his arm looked at their papers one by one before they boarded. The officer watched for a while, then hailed a military car and told me to get in. It seemed to have been waiting for him. He told the driver something in a language that was probably English, and we were whisked off.

The officer asked me how I felt. "Fine," I replied, "except that my legs hurt me and I am hungry."

He said, "Don't worry about it. You will eat very soon."

As we were driving along, it started to snow. The driver switched the windshield wipers on. The regular sound they made reminded me of the noise when the wheels of coal mine wagons or railway cars rolled over a rail joint. It made me sleepy. The officer, sitting on the other side of the car, was smoking again. The smoke of his cigarette was so much more delicate than the smoke of *mahorka* tobacco. It promised perfume and other refined things. I noticed that he only smoked his cigarettes halfway before crushing them. In the train station someone would have picked up the butt, and back in the Donbas no one would have dreamed of throwing half of a cigarette away.

We were riding through a part of the city where the buildings and houses were all destroyed and in shambles. The war must have raged here. The officer didn't say much, and I wondered what he was thinking. Probably, I thought, he wondered what he was doing sitting next to this filthy, stinking creature instead of in his comfortable home.

We must have come close to our destination, because the driver craned his neck, trying to see a street sign. He pulled up to the sidewalk, and the officer said to me, "We're here. Let's get out."

When I looked around, I saw a row of low barracks with a fence around them. *So,* I thought, *this is it.* But we didn't go in that direction. We went into a larger barracks nearby, where a soldier was standing, guarding the entrance. He casually saluted the officer as we went in.

The building was divided in two by a hallway. We walked all the way down the hallway; the officer told me to wait, and he went into an office by himself. There was a bench by the door with blankets on it, and I sat down. The door was only partially closed. I could vaguely hear some voices inside talking in what I was sure was English. The voices went on and on. Maybe they weren't even talking about me. After all, I wasn't that important.

I had closed my eyes and was about to fall asleep when I felt someone standing by me. I opened my eyes and saw a man looking down at me.

"Cum te simts?" he said.

He had asked me in my language how I was feeling! I hadn't heard Romanian spoken for so long that it stunned me.

"I am only very hungry and tired," I replied. I asked him if he spoke English, and he said yes. Then my friend, the officer, came into the hall and motioned me into the office. I got up and went in.

Inside, another man started to tell me about the telegram that was on its way to Romania; he expected a reply within a few hours. He spoke Romanian like a Romanian. Then he asked me about my story, saying that the officer had understood only parts of it. I began to tell him and the other Romanian what I had told the officer, and they translated it.

I asked for some water, and whether I could sit down while I spoke. They told me to sit if I wanted to, and someone gave me a glass of water. I talked about the Donbas and my escape, hoping that I wouldn't have to repeat all this yet again. When I finally finished, I felt drained and exhausted. They kept on talking and talking in English. I asked the first Romanian whether I could go outside into the hallway and lie down on the bench, because I was very tired. He spoke to the officer and then said, "Yes, go ahead and rest."

I had a strange feeling that they thought I would try to run away for fear that the answer to the wire would be negative. If they thought that, they were fools. Where could I run to? What could they do to me, anyway, even if the wire didn't confirm what I had said? Put me in jail? I was telling the truth, and if the wire didn't come I could still write to several people back home.

The floor looked inviting, and I lay down. Heat came from the radiator behind the bench. Within minutes I was asleep. Then someone touched my shoulder. I awoke instantly.

"*A venit telegram,*" one of the Romanians said to me.

"What did it say?" I asked him anxiously.

"*Adevarul* [the truth]," he replied.

I had expected to feel a much greater relief than I actually experienced at that moment.

I had slept for several hours. It was dark outside. I asked the Romanian whether he knew what they intended to do with me now that they knew I had told the truth. He told me I would be taken care of. As soon as the wire had come, the officer who had found me on the train had called some friend of his in an American military hospital. He would see to it that they admitted me there and healed my legs. But I would have to wait a little while longer, for the hospital was near Bremen, which was at least seven hours away by car. If they sent an ambulance for me right away, I would be able to leave by morning.

I couldn't believe that I had become so important that they were going to send an ambulance for me. I would crawl to that hospital if I had to. It sounded just unbelievable to me, a place where I wouldn't have to worry about a thing. Just rest and rest and rest. I asked him whether they would give me food there, too. He grinned and said that no one ate better than they did at that hospital and that I would be well fed. I wondered whether he was lying, but why should he?

The other Romanian and the officer came into the waiting room from the office, and I got up from the floor. The officer came to me and shook my hand while the other Romanian said, "He wants you to know that he is sorry for doubting your story. Since the answer came, he has done everything he could. Now let's go and have something to eat."

They took me to a room behind the office. They had a table there, and an electric stove on which they had started to warm a pot full of *ghiveci,* a Romanian dish made out of all kinds of vegetables. It smelled as only *ghiveci* could smell. When I labeled it correctly as *ghiveci,* they said, "Now we know for sure that you are a Romanian!"

The smell of that dish made me so brutally hungry that I couldn't hold back my tears. The hunger hurt like a burning acid. Finally they gave me a plateful, but I knew that if I ate it very fast I would get sick. So, as hard as it was for me to do it, I carefully ate spoon after spoon.

While I was eating, the two Romanians told me their story. They had been prisoners of war, and they were waiting for repatriation. Yet they were none too anxious to get home, for Romania was still occupied by the Red Army, and the government of the country had changed. No one knew how things really were. Some of their recent letters from home said that the inflation was ruinous. One of them showed me an envelope from a letter he had received only last month. It had at least fifteen stamps on it, and the sum of the stamps ran into thousands of *lei*. The food prices were sky high, and besides that, food was hard to get, no matter what price you paid for it. The price of a meal could go up while you were still eating. The picture they painted of Romania was very different from the one I had been living with for the past two years.

Behind this building there were barracks filled with Romanian ex-soldiers who were also waiting halfheartedly for repatriation. As the two Romanians talked on, I thought some more about the results of war. It seemed that there was nothing left but sad things. The war seemed to have devoured all the warmth, love, and well-being in the world and replaced it with coldness, cruelty, and suspicion. I felt sorry for the two fellows who were talking to me. One of them was from Bucharest, and the other was from Ploesti. They had been soldiers, and now they were stuck in a foreign land. Their families at home were waiting for them and needed them. The repatriations were taking place so slowly that these men didn't seem to know whether to go through with them or not. The rest of the Romanian soldiers in the barracks behind the building were probably in similar situations.

During this time the officer had gone out, and I asked the two Romanians where he had gone and whether they knew anything about him. They told me that he was an American by birth, but of Polish origin. In America he had learned to speak Polish. After the war he had come to work for the Red Cross and the I.R.O., the International Refugee Organization. I asked them whether all the Red Cross personnel were as well dressed as he was, or whether it was only the Americans. They said just the Americans, and that I was lucky because the hospital where I was going was run by Americans and I would be well fed. Just hearing that made my heart fill with pleasure.

Our conversation had become a little warmer. I said that I felt bad having only my Russian pants to wear, because they were so filthy. They told me that some time in the next ten or fifteen hours, my old pants would be burned and I would be given clean pajamas to wear. The word "pajama" struck me as strangely funny. I would wear pajamas? I associated the word with comfort.

The two fellows excused themselves and went to their quarters. They told me to lie down on the sofa in the room and promised to wake me up when the ambulance arrived. As they went out, they turned off the light. I lay still in the dark. As soon as my eyes got used to it, I got up and went to the table, where I found the nearly empty pot of *ghiveci*. I took a spoon and cleaned it out. Then I lay back down on the floor, thinking what a strange day it had been.

Much later I heard someone knock on a door and shout. Then a dog joined in with a deep bark. I wondered whether I had slept long and how far away the morning was. The dog's bark turned into a howl. At home I had seen dogs sit on their haunches and look at the moon and howl. This dog howled and howled until somebody threw something at him and swore. Then it was quiet again.

I was conscious of the throbbing pain in my legs. Some footsteps came into the office. The door to my room opened, and the light went on. The two Romanians were standing at the door. I tried to get up, but my legs were getting worse and worse.

The two fellows grabbed me under the armpits and sat me down on the sofa. "Why didn't you sleep on this?" they asked. I said that it was too soft. They shook their heads. "The ambulance has arrived. From now on, you'd better get used to soft things. This is the time to begin," they teased. Then they asked whether I could walk outside.

"Sure," I said. "Just let me stand up by myself and walk a few steps." With these words I lurched to my feet. I staggered the first few steps, and the pain practically blinded me. But once I got through the office and the waiting room and out into the corridor, I walked straight. I was curious what the American ambulance looked like. From what I had learned about America so far, everything they made was far better than other nations' products.

Outside a waning moon hung overhead. The ambulance was low and only a little larger than a passenger car. It had a red cross painted on the side. As we came to the gate, two men got out of the front seat. One of the two Romanians spoke to them. He went to the back of the ambulance and opened the door. Inside I saw two beds, one on each side, with snow-white sheets on them. The step up into the ambulance was pretty high, and I didn't think I could make it. It hurt, but I got in.

One of the Americans stepped in behind me. He motioned for me to lie down on the bed on the right side, and he put some straps across my chest. From underneath the bed he pulled out a blanket and a pillow. The two Romanians mumbled something to him, and he stepped out. They got in, and one of them told me that he and the Red Cross officer would come along in another car. The other Romanian shook my hand and said that he would find out how my legs were doing from the Red Cross officer. They left. The door was closed, and with a sharp jerk we started out.

Chapter XX

A note to the reader:

When I first wrote this story—and for many years afterward—I was unable to write down what really happened to me at the American hospital. So instead, I wrote what I wished had happened: that I was accepted into the hospital and cared for there. This is what really happened.

WHEN I OPENED my eyes, we were parked in front of a huge building. The sun was shining. Two men were standing next to my stretcher. One of them helped me up. Even though I gritted my teeth, I still felt tears running down my face. I would have fainted if they hadn't gripped me under my arms. I felt terribly helpless. I couldn't understand their language.

Then I got angry at my weakness. I summoned all my will power
and shook off their arms. I could make it. They walked next to me.
We went through a door and down a clean, bright hallway. I didn't
notice much. In fact, the last five or six persons I had met were
blurred in my mind, even the two Romanians. After I had crossed the
border, the sudden loss of a specific goal had numbed my senses.

Now pain and weakness half blinded me. This was a hospital, all
right. The clear, clean smells made my galoshes and pants look and smell
even dirtier. I felt so filthy. A chair was put under me. I started to undo
my galoshes and pants. After I took the bandages off, two doctors
crouched down and looked at the raw, ugly wounds.

They shook their heads and spoke to the Red Cross official. He, in
turn, talked to the Romanian who had come along. My instincts were
alert, but I couldn't understand what they were saying in their foreign
tongue.

Then the Romanian came over to me. In a quiet voice he said,
"They can't keep you here. They say you are too far gone. You might die
in a day or so, and you don't have any papers of identity. But the Red
Cross officer has the address of a refugee camp, and he wants you to go
there. It isn't too far from here, just about five kilometers. He will have
you driven there." He tried to look encouraging as he talked to me, but
I sensed how helpless he felt.

I asked him, "Could I not stay in your camp? You've received the
telegram saying who I am, and you and the Red Cross officer believe me.
I don't think I will die in a day. It's just that I am so tired, so hungry and
dirty."

He sighed, which showed me how he felt, and wiped a tear from his
eyes. "I asked the Red Cross officer, but he can't do it. We are prisoners

of war, and you are a refugee. Our camp is under English Army authority, and they are very strict. So you must go to the refugee camp. But I will try and stay in touch with you. I don't think you will die, either."

I inhaled the clean air, saturated with sharp-smelling medication. Hospital air. After what I had smelled, this was for the gods. Clean white gods for whom you had to have proper papers and be clean even to die.

I started wrapping the pus-soaked bandages on my legs. One of the white-jacketed doctors came over and tried to give me some clean fresh gauze instead. I didn't want it; my pride made me brush the gauze away. I couldn't talk to him, as he was an American, but I wanted to tell him, "Why waste such clean bandages on me? I'm going to die. Just leave me with these dirty rags." He was a physician, but the sight of me didn't do him any good, I could tell from his clean face.

I tightened the rags over my wounds, pulled the heavy, crusty cotton pants over the bandages, and got up. I felt a little dizzy, but I pulled myself together. I couldn't show this doctor any kind of weakness. The Romanian gave me the address of the German refugee camp, saying it was outside Bremen, just down this road to the right. The Red Cross officer said something. He grabbed my arm, but I just kept going, through the heavy door, outside into the fresh cold winter air.

The Romanian came after me. He said that the Red Cross officer wanted me to be driven to the refugee camp. He didn't think I could walk that far.

"I am fine," I said to him. "My legs will have to carry me as far as they can. I would like to be alone now." I shook his hand. "Goodbye. And thank you for the *ghiveci.*" He wiped another tear from his face, and I walked into the morning.

I walked unsteadily along the icy, snowy road, dazed and hungry. The medication I had been given the night before seemed to have made me even more shaky. I wondered what sort of camp this refugee camp would be. For the rest of my life I felt I would be taken from camp to camp, asked questions and more questions. But then, the doctor had said I would die within a day. But I thought that if they would just let me stay in one place for two days, where I could wash my legs and my body, and give me some hot soup, and let me sleep, I would feel fine.

How could I be thinking this way? I must be getting light in the head. I realized I was staggering.

I looked behind me to see if I was being followed. No, there wasn't anybody behind me. No guards with tommy guns slung across their shoulders, no soldiers—nobody. They had told me back there in the hospital that you needed papers to die. Back in the Donbas, if you died, papers weren't necessary.

I was approaching a town. I looked at the address of the refugee camp. Some *Strasse*, it said on it. I stuck it back in my pocket. I didn't feel up to any more questions. I had been alone for so long, I wanted to be alone some more. It was better and safer. Whatever questions I had in my mind I could answer myself.

I felt like sitting down, too tired to walk any further. I saw a giant cement block, square and solid. It looked abandoned; the boardwalk around it was broken up. But there was an entrance, and I headed for it.

It was musty inside the dimly-lit corridor, but the cement floor was dry. Doors led to huge empty rooms. Some had junk in them, cold and musty. I saw a pile of straw in a corner. I lay down on it. I just wanted to rest for a little while.

As I came to my senses again it was dark. I must have fallen asleep. I got up, went outside and urinated, came back and lay down on the straw. My legs felt very sore and swollen, and pus oozed out of the bandages. There was no light, no water, just the stale-smelling straw on the cold hard cement floor.

For the first time I felt really defeated. All through my escape from the Donbas, over the cold barren steppes, I hadn't been so beaten as I was now. In a strange way, I thought about going back, to the camp at Mine 28. There I knew where I belonged, and everybody knew who I was. And there one could die without papers. I couldn't understand it: I had risked everything to escape, and now I missed the camp.

I wanted to see my mother and father once more, but they were far, far away from me.

I dozed for a while. I cried. My legs were devouring me with pain. They stank like a cadaver. It was light again, and dark again, and I became aware of terrible thirst and the ever-present hunger. Outside I found some snow, which I ate, and I went back to the straw. Then I started to tremble. Soon I was shaking so hard my teeth chattered. I tried to stop, but it was impossible....

It was light again. With a great effort I got outside and tried to clean the evil dark-green pus from the foul-smelling bandages in the snow. It was terribly cold. I remembered somebody had told me once that there is acid in urine, or something like that, so back inside I pissed on my wounds to clean them that way. I was degenerating into an animal. I felt as if I was being eaten from the inside by fever and pus, and the hopelessness in my head was drowning me.

Then I pulled myself together. I would try once more before I died.

I found the piece of paper in my pocket and stumbled out of there, continuing down the road where they had told me to look for the refugee camp. I was seeing strange things. Fever was at work, and hunger too had a hand in the flimmering things I saw. Pus squashed in my galoshes as I staggered along the icy road. I started to laugh. No wonder that American doctor had rejected me from his immaculate hospital. To him I must have looked like a piece of garbage. I wondered why they hadn't burnt me, because fire destroys foul smells.

I sat down in the snow, feeling faint. As soon as my body was on the firm ground, I wondered whether I would be able to get up again and make it back to Mine 28, where I would know where I was. Was I heading back there or wasn't I? I didn't remember what I had decided to do. Ahh, the best thing would be to sleep....I rubbed some snow in my face to get me out of the mental morass. I was near croaking. It wasn't as bad as one would expect it to be.

I saw some houses not far away. I looked at the sky. It was grey. It would snow soon. My friend the snow. I gobbled down a mouthful. It was good, cool and fresh. I took another mouthful. How much better to die in clean white snow than to suffocate in a black coal mine.

But I didn't want to die!

All of a sudden I wanted to get to the refugee camp, to try once more. I hadn't done anything. I might not be good enough for a nice clean American hospital, but I might still be considered a sort of human being, the kind they let into a refugee camp.

It took me a while until I was on my feet again. It was very hard. There wasn't much strength left. I knew the last days in that cement bunker had completely exhausted my reserves. As I staggered along, I realized that even if I had tried I could never have made it back to the Donbas. I was too far gone.

Things were dancing in front of my eyes. I felt as heavy as lead. I wanted so much to lie down and never move again. I was just too tired...too tired....

I pitched into the hard-packed snow of the road.

Chapter XXI

THERE WAS MOVEMENT, motion. I was aware that all kinds of things were going on, and somehow I was the center. I didn't want to be the center of anything. I just wanted to be left alone.

I didn't feel the pain in my legs, but still there was activity. I thought I even felt my clothes being taken from me. I wanted to get out of the dark. The clothes that I had were the only thing I owned, and now they were taking them from me, too. Maybe they wanted me to die naked, so I would be cold to the very last. I was so worthless, now I had forfeited the right to my clothes. As long as they didn't beat me, just let me die in peace. I didn't want to feel or think any more....

I opened my eyes. A young, grey-haired, kind face was bent over me, looking at my chest, then at my face. I wanted to move my legs, but I couldn't. A cold shock went through me, ice-cold. It seared through me in a flash: my legs had been cut off!

The kind face took the blanket off from over my body. I raised my head and saw…my legs! They were tied down with a blanket. What relief! I still had my legs.

Then I remembered the hard-packed road I had been walking on. I had fallen down, I remembered that much. Someone must have found me. I probably was in the refugee camp. There was a thick bandage on my legs, both of them. I was a little cleaned up, in a room with four beds on either side, cots, like in the army. But it was clean.

"Ich bin ein Arzt," the gray-haired man began. "I am a doctor." He told me that I was in the refugee camp, that I had been found on the road not far from the camp. "We will save your legs," he continued, "but you can't move for about ten days. We will feed you here as best we can. Then when you feel better and your legs are in better condition, you tell us how you came here, and from where."

I tried to thank him, but he said, "No, no. Just rest now." With that he left the room.

Within minutes another young fellow came in with a large bowl of steaming soup. The aroma hit me with a terrible impact. It was a thick turnip brew. The young man left me alone. I inhaled the brew's steam. Ahh, it made me dizzy! I started slurping it little by little, then I picked the bowl up and drank it. I wanted more.

Way back in my mind I remembered a doctor in a white jacket who had said I would die within a day or so. Well, with this turnip brew inside of me, his diagnosis would be faulty. The hot brew was swilling around in my stomach, and I felt it manufactured new hope and strengthened the will to live.

Later that day I got several plates of the same brew. I looked around at the refugees who shared my room. They were all young lads, skinny and quiet. They didn't say much, not even to one another. The gray-haired doctor came by towards evening, and he showed me a pot with a cover that I was to use if I needed to urinate, etc. He brought a wash-bowl, mopped my face, and wished me good night. I slept like the dead.

In the back of my mind I knew I was safe, that I was among human beings. From the surroundings they didn't have much, but they gave what they had. I will be grateful until the day I die for that gray-haired young doctor. He was a royal human being.

Days after coming to consciousness in that camp, I learned what the doctor had done. He had taken some blood out of my vein, and stirred it till the parts that coagulate were separated from the serum. Then he had dipped some gauze into the serum and laid it on my wounds. After ten days, when he removed the bandages, the ugliness and red angriness of the wounds was gone. Of course they were still very sore, and the doctor said I was to be gentle with my walking—and absolutely no running. He saw to it that I was given two bowls of turnip brew at every meal. The other refugees, for some reason, didn't like it too much. I couldn't get enough of it.

The big relief was that after the bandages were removed, I could get into the showers. Of course there wasn't any hot water, but there was plenty of cold, and I showered till I was blue. The doctor, whose name was Gustav, was amazed that the cold water didn't bother me. "Water is water," I told him. "Cold water washes the dirt off just as well, you just have to scrub a little harder." He had given me a nice piece of soap—American soap, he whispered. He also told me that I would heal much faster if I could have more sugar, fats, fresh meat, and fruits, "but those things only the Americans have." I didn't say anything. I hadn't told him about being thrown out of the American hospital.

By then I *had* told Dr. Gustav from where I had escaped, and of the harsh living conditions I had left behind me. "I know something of those conditions," he said. "I was on the front lines in Russia, in 1944. Their winters aren't alien to me, and those endless steppes." He shook his head. "I can't understand how you survived," he said quietly. "Your constitution defies the medical laws." Then he put his hand on my head, saying, "You don't know yet what you have accomplished. But in the years to come, when you look back, you will realize."

The way I felt at that moment, I would gladly have changed places with almost anybody so that I wouldn't have to remember what was behind me. I thought constantly about Omar, and some of the others, because in dreams they were with me, and I felt that it would be so for a while.

It had started after about two weeks in the refugee camp. And as dreams are, no matter what I dreamed about, Omar was in the dream, whether the setting was the refugee camp, or on one of the escape trains, or even the American hospital...

The American military police were beating us with clubs and fists. Omar didn't want me to fight back, because of my legs, but I struggled against him holding me back. Then, strangely, we were both handcuffed. Omar's wrists started to bleed as he struggled against the cuffs. They hit us on our heads with clubs, and one of them kicked me on my leg. I howled with pain, and then they threw us out. We were going back to the Donbas, back to the camp at Mine 28...

The relief was great when I woke up drenched with perspiration. It was very hard to go back to sleep after those dreams. But then day would come, and the turnip brew, and visits and small talk with Dr. Gustav. My roommates, mostly young East Germans, brought daily bits of information and happenings from the thriving black market that had sprung up in the ruins of occupied Germany—a makeshift economy where the American cigarette was king, preferred to any kind of currency. I noticed them wearing black clothes, made of a strong, warm material, which they told me were discarded American Army uniforms dyed black. I couldn't believe the Americans had thrown them out. What wouldn't I have given to have clothing like that in Russia!

I had ample time to observe the comings and goings of the shiftiest refugees, the ones who had the best deals going for them on the black market. But all too soon it would become dark, another plate or two of turnip brew, and the night was there...

I was sitting in the Golovoi's office. A Russian miner whose name I couldn't remember, though his face was very familiar from the level where Omar and I worked, had brought me a black suit, a black shirt, a black tie, black shoes and a black fur cap. From his pocket he pulled some black footrags, partyanki, and a coil of string to tie them. I wondered, why had he brought me these clothes, which were much too fine to work in the mine? As I pondered this, the Golovoi came in. "Get dressed, Vanya," he said. "Everybody is waiting for you. You are the last." The words sent a chill through me.

He went out, and absentmindedly I started dressing. The clothes fitted well, except that the shirt collar was too large. I realized I had a very skinny neck. Then I wrapped my feet up in the footrags, carefully, so they wouldn't touch my wounds. As I was tying them with string, I realized that my legs and feet were clean. I was confused. How had I gotten so clean?

I walked outside. From the Golovoi's office to the mine, all the coal miners were lined up, all dressed in black, and they carried coffins on their shoulders. The workers had their mine clothes on and their faces were also black, as if they had just come out of the mine. But a few of the foremen, including Sirienko, the Golovoi, *and the man who ran the machine shop, had on black suits like the one they had given me. Everyone who had on a black suit had a clean face.*

As I stood looking at this procession, Sirienko came over to me. His face was tired and drawn, and I noticed that the deep frown lines all over his face still had coal dust in them. He asked me how my legs were, but instead of replying I asked him, "Why all the coffins? I see almost every Russian miner here, but nobody from the camp. Why?"

"Vanya," he said, "you are the only one left alive."

"But where will all these prisoner be buried?" I asked him. "There are so many." The miners were carrying them slowly past us, and more and more kept appearing. They came from behind the stalova, *and up there by the tower and the* atkatka *the miners were picking the coffins up.*

Sirienko said, "We have an order that you have to take every one of them up on the tower and dump them out."

"But how can I do that?" I protested. "You know that every coffin will shatter to pieces when they fall on the poroda *rocks. And the bodies will start to smell after several days."*

"Vanya, we have this order, and they are waiting for you to start. So let's go. If the bodies start to smell we'll do something about it later." But I knew nothing would be done.

Sirienko and I walked towards the atkatka *and the piled-up coffins. The miners were terribly gloomy, the* Golovoi *stood quietly on the side, and the captain and several other officers stood waiting for the burial ceremonies to begin. I was frightened to see the grinning face of the sadistic guard who had twice nearly killed me. What was he doing here? Hadn't the captain ordered him transferred, and even threatened to shoot him if he ever saw him here again?*

Two guards loaded a coffin into the wagon and pushed me towards it. I stepped up, the winch operator was given a sign, and I was on the way up. I wondered who was in this coffin. As I looked at it, riding up and up, I noticed that the lumber of the coffin looked moldy, like braces that have been in the mine for a long time.

Near the top of the tower I yelled to stop. The wagon stopped, and I released the safety and tipped the wagon. The coffin fell out. Falling it turned slowly, and then CRASH...it struck the rocks and splintered, and the body of a prisoner fell from rock to rock. Rolling down, it was mutilated beyond recognition.

I put the wagon back, fastened the safety, and raised my arm in the signal to roll down. Another coffin was loaded onto the wagon, and up again. Slowly but surely I unloaded them all.

The last coffin was larger than all the others. On the way up, I realized that this must be Omar. I wondered how he had died. Then I was on top of the tower, and as I dumped the coffin out, I felt like jumping after it. The first impact smashed the coffin, and Omar's body, still clad in his mining clothes, rolled out. But to my horror, Omar clutched the next rock he fell on. He turned his head towards me, blood streaming from his face, and as I leaned out to jump, he screamed, "Don't do it! Don't do it!..."

I woke up screaming.

For a long time I dreaded falling asleep. Those dreams terrified me. After a while I wasn't so scared of the life I had escaped from in the Donbas; I was frightened of the white-jacketed doctor from the American hospital. I knew it wasn't reasonable, but it was very real. My legs were healing; the wounds were growing smaller every day, and there was hardly any pain left. But now it seemed as if the infection was in my mind.

One day the doctor brought me some paper and said, "It would be good if you would write your parents a letter. Tell them your legs are healing nicely, and for the time being you are under a roof and being looked after. Give me the letter, address the envelope, and I will put a stamp on it and mail it for you." This Dr. Gustav was a real human being, for he had given me his own pen.

Slowly, unused to writing with my mine-calloused hands, I wrote a letter home, sitting on the bed. It was a letter I had thought about writing for some time. It was strange to write, simply because when I had seen my parents the last time, I had been a young, foolish kid. In the last three years I had changed, I thought. I had gone through the mire of life, and those things leave their marks. I wondered what the last three years had done to them, how they had managed. These insane times must have been hard on them as well.

Almost two weeks had passed when one morning at about eleven o'clock Dr. Gustav came in with a letter in his hand. It was in a blue envelope that I immediately recognized as my father's stationery. As far back as I remembered, he had used those blue envelopes. I took it from the doctor, and he left the room, sensing that I wanted to be alone when I read it.

On the back of the envelope I saw thousands of *lei* stamps. There must have been terrible inflation in Romania. In other times it had taken a 7 lei stamp to send a letter anywhere in the world. I opened the letter carefully and took out two pages, one from my father, one from my mother.

I read the letter, then I read it again. My sister, two years older than me, had died in a Russian camp at Makeyevka, just 50 kilometers from where I had been in the Donbas. She had been taken from home a few weeks after I was picked up on the street, and had succumbed, like so many prisoners that first winter, less than six months after our arrest. My parents had been notified of this by the authorities. I was their only child now. For two long years, they had been hoping for a sign of life from me.

My father was very strong in his words. The worst was behind me, he said. I was a strong man now, and I would go forth into life and make it. He only felt badly about not being able to help me. But his spirit was with me, and I should not forget that. "You have survived," he said. "You must remain free. You cannot risk coming home until it is safe. Your mother and I long to see you, but for the time being, we are happy just knowing you are alive." He meant well, the old patriarch. God, I missed him.

Then my mother went on with the endless questions only a mother can ask a son: did I have enough to eat, and the clothes I needed? How much did I weigh? Did I sleep well? How bad was my leg injury really?—and so on. They included the address of that uncle of mine who was a doctor here in Germany somewhere. I was to look him up, and he would look after me and my legs.

All sorts of feelings swept through me. I felt raw and sore inside and happy at the same time. I put the letter under my mattress and lay down. I would want to read it again and again. I hadn't realized how much I had missed my parents. In the Russian camp I had not allowed myself that weakness.

I still saw my father in front of me when I had been locked in the boxcar, and I had shown him confidence in my face, so that he would know I would be able to take care of myself. His face had been near the breaking point at that moment. Yes, it must have been very hard on such a strong man. I wondered how and when I would ever see him again, and whether I would find him bent with age and misery, like a giant tree gnarled by fighting the strong winds.

And my sister. As kids we had had our battles, but we had a lot of fun together, and I loved her. For the first time in a long time, I reminisced about our childhood. I had been the better swimmer, but she had been an excellent diver, and she had often teased me about being afraid to dive from higher than ten feet. She was fearless. What if we had known what lay in store for both of us? The sad part was that she had died not far from me in Russia. If only she had been in my camp at Mine 28! I would have helped her as best I could, but it would have been very difficult. I might have married one of the Russian girls to be able to get more food for her. What would have happened to her while I was in the hospital? Certainly I could not have escaped alone, leaving her in the camp. But it was too late for such thoughts. I hoped she hadn't suffered too much.

As sad as I was, lying on that bed I felt different. I had more confidence now, more strength. The mere fact that I could communicate with my father again was what a strong wind is to a sailor drifting on a windless sea. He is exhausted from paddling, trying to move his boat, but as the sails fill with wind, his chest fills with hope, and the journey continues.

I wrote to my parents the next day and told them not to write to me at this camp any more, but to write me in care of my uncle. Somehow I would get to him. And I discussed with Dr. Gustav the possibility of getting transferred to another camp. I wanted to get into the center of Bremen, where I felt I could orient myself better I didn't mention it to Dr. Gustav, who would have worried about my legs, but I was eager to get involved in the black-market trading. There was a DP (Displaced Persons) camp in Bremen, and within a week I was on a bus to that camp.

There the Red Cross officer found me again, bringing the same young Romanian along as an interpreter. I sensed that he still felt guilt about not being able to get me into the hospital. I showed him the freshly healed scars on my legs and told him I was doing fine. He gave me five packs of American cigarettes, even though he knew I didn't smoke. He must have been aware of the fact that on the black market it represented great wealth, especially for someone as poor as I was. It became my starting capital.

The Red Cross officer talked to me constructively about my life. His opinion was that I should get out of warsick Europe as soon as possible, and so he helped me get into Transit Camp Buchholz, outside of Hannover, from which a steady stream of DPs emigrated to Canada, Australia, and the United States.

By that time, of course, I had heard all kinds of wonder tales from the other blackmarketeers about America, the Horn of Plenty that poured forth chocolate bars, cigarettes, coffee, and other treasures onto the black market from its soldiers' PXes. America was helping to feed hundreds of thousands of DPs, too. What kind of abundance must there be in a country that could afford that? In America, I thought, I would be safe. Hunger couldn't get to me. But to go to the United States, you needed a relative there, and I didn't have any. I decided to set my sights on Canada. From there, perhaps, I could get into the United States.

Lying on my bunk in Camp Buchholz, surrounded by thousands of other refugees waiting for a chance to go to the New World, I allowed myself to dream. Once my legs healed completely, I thought I would be stronger than a well-trained athlete. I would ask the Americans to let me work in one of their coal mines. They must be much better and safer than Russian coal mines. I was a good miner. I would work very hard, and they would like me—I would save my earnings, and perhaps they would let me bring my mother and father to America. I hadn't done anything wrong, they should let me do that, it wouldn't hurt anybody. I fell asleep.

The End

Epilogue

IF I ENDED my story here, it would leave many questions unanswered. Indeed, when I first wrote the story down, in 1958, I did not know the answers myself. Had Omar survived? If so, would we ever find each other again? And then, what about my mother and father? Separated from each other by the "Iron Curtain," would life allow us to be reunited? And last, would I ever return to Russia, to the Donbas?

In 1949, I succeeded in emigrating to Canada. There I first worked on a logging railroad in the wild Ontario forest, and then trained as a heavyweight fighter in Montréal. A promoter from Chicago became interested in me, and my fists fulfilled my dream of coming to live in the United States. Then, in the midst of a promising professional fight career, I was drafted. In 1955, as a soldier in the U.S. Army stationed in Europe, I became an American citizen.

But even as a new U.S. citizen, I did not dare to go back to Romania to see my parents. In the 1950s and early 1960s there was no diplomatic relationship between the United States and the Soviet Bloc countries. Had the Communists chosen to keep me, or to punish me for escaping, the American government could have done nothing to help me. And so it happened that I never saw my father again. Though we wrote to each other often, that glimpse through the small window of the boxcar taking me away to the Donbas was to be our last sight of each other.

As wealthy landowners before the war, my parents had had everything taken from them by the Communists. They were allowed to continue living in two rooms of the spacious house where I grew up, but only as tenants, and strangers were moved into the rest of the house. My mother was made to scrub floors in a hospital, and my father, who had been a respected power in our whole region, was put to work in a clay factory. I learned much later that he was severely questioned by the *Securitate,* the Romanian equivalent of the dreaded Russian KGB, about my supposed "spy" activities. In 1960, my father became ill with cancer. "Don't come," he commanded me in his letters. My freedom and safety was more important than seeing my face before he died. In 1961 I received a telegram from my mother: "Your father passed away peacefully."

In the letters I wrote to my parents, which I knew were opened and read by the *Securitate,* I had never dared to ask about Omar, even though his grandfather had once lived across the street from us and they could probably have learned about his fate. Also, I was afraid to hear bad news. I didn't know how anyone, even Omar, could have survived the hard labor and cold winters much longer with so little food and no warm clothing. And then there were always cave-ins to worry about. In spite of everything, could he still be alive? Not knowing, Omar continued to haunt my dreams and nightmares.

A song that became popular in America in the early '60s hit me with force when I heard it. It was called "Big Bad John" and was sung by a country singer named Jimmy Dean: The song was about a big, powerful coal miner who was a mystery to the other miners. He never said more than "Hi." Nobody got close to him. And then there was a terrible accident in the mine. Hundreds of men were trapped deep underground. But silent Big John lifted up a beam with the strength of Samson, enabling all the men to escape—all but him.

Had Omar saved my life only to perish in the mine himself?

With the Khrushchev era, the Cold War began to thaw a little. Diplomatic ties were established between the U.S. and Romania. By 1965 or '66 we had an embassy there, and I could begin to consider going back to see my mother. I was now the owner of a popular jazz bar in Greenwich Village, "Jacques." (By the way, that's not the name my mother gave me. It's the name the Russian lieutenant gave me with a pair of boots. "Vanya" in Russian would become "Johnny" to the American soldiers in postwar Germany, "Jack" when I was fighting professionally, and "Jacques" when I studied in Paris after the army. But it's all the same name in different languages—I'm still Vanya.) One night I just made an impulsive decision to go home.

My plane to Vienna made a stop in Frankfurt, and I got off there and sent my mother a telegram. I was afraid the shock of suddenly seeing me might be too much for her. I wanted to give her a day to prepare herself. In Vienna I rented a car and drove eastward without stopping— a drive of seventeen hours. The worst part was crossing the "Iron

Curtain" at the border between Austria and Hungary. The grim armed guards, the watchtowers flanked by triple-strand barbed wire, the long, tense questioning by the border patrol, the atmosphere of fear and total control—I couldn't believe I was voluntarily going back into the nightmare I had escaped from.

It was dawn when I drove into my home village. The houses, so proud and well-kept in my childhood, now looked drab, neglected and broken-down. Communism had done a lot of damage. And our old house, where my mother still lived—it was dark! Why wasn't she waiting up for me? Was she alive?

I got out of the car and threw a handful of pebbles against the window. Nothing. I picked up a stick and tapped. The curtain was pushed back, and in the window appeared the face of an old woman—my mother. It had been twenty-two years.

On her face was an expression of such shock I thought she would have a heart attack. I ran to the front gate that led to the courtyard. In a moment I heard the key rattling in the lock as her hands trembled. Then she pulled open the door in the gate and we stood staring at each other.

"Didn't you get my telegram?" I asked her—in English!

"Can't you speak your language any more?" she asked me. And then we were in each other's arms. (The telegram finally arrived at five o'clock that evening!)

From then on, I visited my mother every year, often twice a year, for the rest of her life—sixteen more years. I longed to bring her to America, but Communist Romania did not permit its citizens to travel or emigrate. Still, we spent weeks together, living under the same old roof, driving in the mountains, getting up in the middle of the night to drink tea at the kitchen table and talk. We told each other stories of our lives since we were parted and healed some of the wounds left by the lost years. My mother said that my wife, Annie, consoled her for the loss of my sister. We were with her, holding her hands, when she died at age 84, in the same bed where she had given birth to me.

On my very first visit to my mother, I had asked her if she knew anything about Omar, whose grandfather had once lived right across the street. She hadn't heard anything. I didn't trust anyone else enough to ask. And so I left Romania that first time, and the second time too, without knowing the fate of my friend.

It was my third trip. I had just driven my mother back from a visit with some friends when a neighbor, an elderly woman, told me that a man had been at the house asking for me. He had not left a name, but had said he would come back soon.

My mother and I were sitting in the kitchen, eating and reminiscing. The kitchen window faced the street and an old tree with low branches in front of the house. I was looking out at that tree, remembering how I used to climb it as a kid, when I saw the legs of a man walking toward our house. The low-hanging branch hid the upper part of his body. I had seen that light, ambling walk before—only very strong men walk that way. I ran out the front door—and there was Omar.

It is impossible to describe the emotions that went through both of us as we stood there facing each other after all those years. The coal mine, the bitter cold, the gnawing hunger, the despair of the camp—they hadn't been able to kill him. Here he was, ruddy and healthy. We grabbed each other's hands and then embraced.

He told me that he had known of my successful escape. I had written from West Germany to a friendly guard in our camp, asking him to let Omar know I was safe, and the letter had actually arrived. Omar himself had been one of the last few men left alive in that camp. He had survived three more years. I will never know how he made it through the first two. His last year, the few surviving prisoners had received more food and better clothing. At last they had been allowed to go home.

We went for a drive together and filled each other in on all that had happened in our lives since we last saw each other in the field hospital in Rovenki more than twenty years before. Omar was now an engineer in an important position. He had built his house with his own hands, and dug his own well. We drove there so I could meet his wife and daughter. His wife drew on their meager resources to cook the kind of meal he and I had dreamed of in the mine long ago. Over that dream dinner we talked about the possibility of his visiting me one day in New York City. Omar couldn't believe that it would ever happen.

On the way back to my mother's house, I told him that I had written and published a book about our life in the Donbas, a book I had dedicated to him. Back at the house, I gave him a copy of the story you have just read. It looked very small in his huge hand. Omar looked at me and asked a shattering question: "You told it all in *this* little book?"

From then on, every time I visited my mother I spent time with him, too.

Vanya and Omar in Romania, about 1980

We never spoke much about the mine; we didn't have to. There were memories of misery that only the two of us knew. When the subject did come up, Omar would just look at me and say, "Let it be."

After my mother died, I began fighting to get Omar out of Romania. His daughter married in the 1980s and managed to get out to West Germany, where her husband had relatives. Omar and his wife wanted to join her there. Their government adamantly refused to let them go. Finally, with the help of a friend in the U.S. State Department, I was able to win his freedom. Omar made his new home in West Germany, and in 1989, I flew him and his wife to New York and then to Florida. When I met Omar at Kennedy Airport, I reminded him how he had scoffed that this would never happen! In New York we visited the

Statue of Liberty; in Florida we had a barbecue on the beach in our
bathing suits—a scene that, in the dark depths of Mine 28, we could
never have imagined in our wildest dreams.

One dream was never to be. I had always wanted to go back to the
Donbas someday—with Omar. Unfortunately, he was already suffering
from heart disease when he visited me in the spring of 1989. That fall
and winter, Communism ceased to be, holding out the hope that one
day soon we would be able to revisit the Donbas safely. But Omar died
suddenly of a massive heart attack in 1991 Once again I was alone with
my memories.

It wasn't until 1999 that I was invited, as International Advisor to
the International Karate Organization Kyokushinkai-kan, to the
European Karate Championships in Kiev, the capital of Ukraine. The
breakup of the Soviet Union had placed the Donbas within the far eastern reaches of Ukraine, and I decided that, ready or not, this was my
chance to go. When the tournament was over, I took a small propeller
plane from Kiev to Donetsk, the capital of the coal-mining region.
Imagine my reaction when I saw "DONBAS" written on the side of the
airplane in large orange letters!

Donetsk is a fairly big city. Next to it lies Makeyevka, where my
poor sister died. To find the remote and barren landscape where I had
worked, I had to hire a car and driver—and an interpreter, for my
Russian was very rusty—and drive eastward for several hours, stopping
frequently to ask the way. When we had driven about halfway, looking
out the window I felt a shock in my heart. After fifty-two years, I was
looking at a *tiricon*, a *poroda* hill and tower exactly like the one I had
worked on: a black cone with a bit of railroad track extending beyond

its tip. You might say it looked sinister, jutting up above that flat landscape like a small black pyramid or an extinct volcano, but to me it looked like an old friend. My job on just such a tower had helped save my life. I wanted to reach out to it.

Finally we came to the small villages and the town where my Russian friends at Mine 28 had lived: Venherovka, Mikhailovka, Rovenki. But I recognized nothing. A lot changes in fifty-two years. Where was the *atkatka,* the bathhouse, the *stalova?* I could not orient myself. By asking at the office of a new mine, we learned that Mine 28, once the best coal producer in the Donbas, had long since been mined out and closed. Where the mine entrance had been, there was now a shoe factory, also closed. But a kind lady offered to take us there. And so I saw what must have been *my* poroda hill. It was no longer in use and was becoming an ordinary hill, with a few small trees growing on it. Just a few blackened posts stuck out, the remains of Sirienko's tower.

I told our guide, Lyudmila, about the Russian girls I had worked with. I knew them only as Lisa, Nina, Katya, Dusya. I had never known their family names. Lyudmila said she would take us to an old woman who might know. On the way to the old woman's house, we passed a high, open meadow that Lyudmila told me was where the prison camp barracks had been. With no buildings or other familiar landmarks, I couldn't be sure. I didn't recognize it. But it was very moving to see that the local Russians had refrained from building anything on that ground where so many of us prisoners had lived—and died. That's not quite correct: they had built one thing. At the front of the field is a small monument, with a hollow-eyed face, a hand holding barbed wire, and the words, "To All the Prisoners of War." We had never been forgotten.

The old woman, Klavdia, was my age, but looked ten or fifteen years older. The coal miners of the Donbas, men and women, had lived an unforgiving life. Yes, Klavdia had known Lisa, Nina, and Katya. And she knew Lisa and Nina were dead. She wasn't sure about Katya. But Dusya—the fiery Dusya was still very much alive. Would I like to see her?

We drove up to a neat small house. Children were playing across the dirt road. A little old woman with sparkling eyes came out of the house. I looked at the old woman. I would never have recognized her if I'd passed her on the street. She had only a few teeth left, and she was shorter than I remembered. But those proud, high cheekbones...

"Dusya," Lyudmila said, "do you remember a prisoner named Vanya?"

The old woman looked at me. She picked up the corners of her apron and wiped tears from her eyes. "Vanyushka! Vanyushka!" she said.

The next year, in May 2000, after a karate tournament in Russia, I returned to the Donbas. From Lyudmila I learned that another old woman who had worked at Mine 28 had heard about my last visit and wanted to see me. Did I remember a Marusya?

Marusya—my shift supervisor on the *atkatka!* While Dusya always had a friendly word for me, we had never worked together. But with Marusya I had worked closely every day the whole summer I was on the tower. When she came out of her gate, I recognized her at once— her strong, sad beauty—and she knew me, too. Strangest of all, I began speaking fluent Russian with her, as if we were resuming a conversation we had left off yesterday—but "yesterday" was 54 years ago. It was such a shock that I had a high fever for a day.

For her lifetime of hard work in the mines, Marusya Kozlova had been "rewarded" by the bankrupt Ukrainian government with a pension of about ten dollars a month. She was taking care of a husband with Alzheimer's disease alone in a house with no running water. (Her husband died not long after our visit.) And yet she was strong and cheerful. I cannot repay the kindness of Sirienko, who died many years ago, or of the simple Russians who fed and sheltered me during my escape at great risk to themselves. But perhaps I can now repay a little of the all-important encouragement Marusya and the other Russian girls gave me.

Next time, I will take her to the place where Mine 28 used to be and ask her: "Marusya, *pokazhi menye*—show me. Where was the *atkatka?* the *stalova?* Where was the bathhouse, the *banya?* Where did the ladders come out of the ground, and where was the *uklon* where the full coal cars rumbled out of the mine to the sad sound of the *libyotka?*" Only then will I truly have returned to the Donbas.

Printed in the United States
3801